MW00444984

Thinking My Way to the End of the World

A Memoir

Jerry Waxler

Neuralcoach Press
PO Box 99
Quakertown, PA 18951

ISBN: 978-0-9771895-7-1
Book Cover Design: Maciej Krzywicki

Disclaimer

All facts have been presented as accurately as possible. Dialog reproduces the tone and content of the conversation, to the best of the author's ability. All descriptions of beliefs are based on his own interpretation. In some cases, names of individuals and details of groups have been changed or obscured in order to protect privacy.

Becoming a Man

Philadelphia, Bar Mitzvah Day, 1960

I clutched the arms of my chair as men in robes slid open the doors of the ornate tabernacle. They cradled the holy Torah in their arms, removed its lavishly embroidered cover and embossed silver breastplate, and set it on a table. Each step brought me closer to the part I would have to play. For years, I sat among the congregation watching this ritual. Today, in the month of my thirteenth birthday, I was the one who would be watched. My mouth was dry. I felt small and inconsequential. I hoped no one could see me.

They unrolled the scrolled parchment and read from it in voices so filled with emotion I thought they might cry. I wanted to cry, too. I had attended dozens of practice sessions, during which I tried to memorize the string of Hebrew syllables that were supposed to turn me from a boy into a man. But like most things related to synagogue, I had barely paid attention.

On the rabbi's cue, I forced myself to approach the table. Could he see how frightened I was? He gestured with his silver pointer to my place in the Torah. I stared at the ancient script, decorated with crowns and squiggles far more cryptic than the Hebrew alphabet printed in our prayer books.

Sweat moistened my forehead. I tried to remember how to turn these symbols into sounds. The rabbi whispered a phrase to get me started. I sputtered his suggestion, my voice not much louder than his. Then I stopped, numb with terror. Phrase by phrase, we pressed on, him whispering and me squeaking. When it was over, I slunk back to my chair.

Instead of announcing to the world that I was now a man, this ritual showed that I had no idea what that even meant.

§§§

Synagogue seemed like a distraction from my real mission — to succeed in public school. And I was about to enter the next phase in that journey. Central High drew the smartest, most ambitious boys in Philadelphia. My father had attended. And so had my brother. Now it was my turn.

Since students traveled here from every neighborhood, I didn't recognize a single boy in my homeroom class. But on the first day, I received exciting news. I must have scored high on my aptitude tests because even though my grades in junior high were not at the top, I was placed in an honors class with the thirty boys deemed the smartest of the smart. Along with the honor came pressure. I needed to prove I belonged there.

In each classroom, I pondered the weight of the material, as my briefcase grew so heavy I thought I might tip over. The most interesting subject was algebra, taught by Mr. Abrams. His enormous personality exploded from his five-foot frame, and his Brooklyn accent made him sound more Jewish than anyone I knew. His entire being seemed focused on forcing us to learn as much algebra as possible.

At the start of each class, he dared us to come to the front of the room. "Come on, you lazy bums. Let's see what you can do," he said, his gravelly voice dripping with mock sarcasm. When he nodded at me, I left the safety of my chair. Trembling with excitement, I grasped the cold, hard chalk in my fingers, heard the clatter and scratch of my equation appearing on the board, felt the eyes of thirty strangers on the back of my head.

When I finished, I turned to him. His eyes softened. "Good work," he said, his sneer replaced by a smile. I was thrilled to please him, and equally delighted that my classmates had seen my performance. I absorbed each new lesson, its esoteric symbols offering me a chance to solve the problem and win the prize.

§§§

In the hall between classes, we honors students clung together, challenging each other in a series of impromptu quizzes. Someone would toss out an obscure word and whoever defined it correctly, won. To survive that game, I bought a deck of vocabulary flashcards and studied them every evening. Over time, I became pretty good. "What is hirsute?" someone asked. I dove in like a catcher scooping up a line drive. "Hairy." Someone else called out, "What is pejorative?" I knew that one, too. "A negative judgment." For those moments, I felt good about myself. I belonged.

But between each question, I was gripped by uncertainty. In the honors class, you were only as smart as your last answer.

When I wasn't studying, or worrying about schoolwork, or trying to impress the other boys, I spent every spare minute reading. On the trolley to and from school, soothed by the swaying and the sound of scraping metal on the tracks, I lost myself in books about traveling to outer space. On Sunday evenings, when Dad took the family out to dinner, I kept a book next to my plate, ready to steal a moment in the author's make-believe world.

Despite my love for reading and my expanding repertoire of obscure words, English class bored me. While the teacher droned on about some grammar lesson, I glanced at the novel stashed under my desk. Once I became immersed in a story about a group of terrified teenagers who were colonizing a planet in some faraway galaxy. A shadow came over me and I crashed back to earth. My teacher's pale skin shone crimson. He grabbed the book from me. "How dare you?" he asked, his voice trembling. His disgust lingered throughout the year.

Despite receiving a C in first-year English, my excellent vocabulary landed me back in the honors section in the second year, where the reading assignments grew more complex. One day, the teacher read *Ode: Intimations of Immortality,* a poem by William Wordsworth.

When he asked us to interpret it, hands shot up, but not mine. He called on me anyway. "What do you think it means, Waxler?"

"I don't know," I said, hating myself for my ignorance. *What does he mean by, "What does it mean?"*

He called on another student who eagerly answered. "The phrase 'Some little plan or chart' means the baby's future is already spelled out. The poem is about life following some sort of plan." The teacher smiled. The other student looked pleased, and I felt left out. *How did he know that?*

I spent all my energy at Central trying to convince people I was smart, and if I failed, I felt like an idiot. I kept trying, though. I had no choice. If I wasn't smart, I was nothing.

Seeking My Identity in the New World

By the time I turned sixteen, instead of going to synagogue on Saturday mornings, I began a new ritual. Each week I took the subway to Center City Philadelphia. When I emerged into the subdued light of the City Hall courtyard, I stood beneath the statue of William Penn, the founder of Pennsylvania. My body tingled, as if I had traveled through a wormhole into history.

William Penn's name echoed like a holy legend in my mostly Jewish public school, where almost all of us had grandparents who fled violent attacks on Jewish villages. Our lives depended on the idealism of those founders who had defended freedom of religion. And since I grew up in the city where it all began, I wanted to reach back in time and thank those characters who had created this safe haven.

Some days I walked toward Independence Hall where, just a century after Penn founded the colony, a band of revolutionaries broke away from the king. Walking these streets made me feel just a whisper away from their discussions about the Declaration of Independence.

Ben Franklin stood out as one of the most magnificent of these heroes. In addition to helping found the nation, his contributions to its culture played an important part in my life. He founded the first lending library in the colonies, so I thought of him every time I walked up the Ben Franklin Parkway to the main branch of the Free Library of Philadelphia. Its massive, classic columns and vast high-ceilinged study rooms made it seem like the cultural center of the world.

The University of Pennsylvania was another product of Ben Franklin's creative genius. When my history teacher assigned a research report about the Pullman Strike of 1894, he said the best place to find information was at the University's library. On the beautiful, tree-lined campus, among ancient buildings, I entered the library's musty stacks. Passing college students studying in their carrels, I located old books related to the deadly confrontation between soldiers and workers.

I was horrified by what I learned. Little more than a century after the American Revolution that granted us freedom from the king's tyranny, our own government sent in troops to break up a strike. I felt a chill of fear when I realized that even in our safe country, the government could turn against its own people. The research helped me understand why workers needed to organize unions in order to force business owners to take care of them. It appeared that defense against tyranny required ongoing effort.

My connection to the university took a new turn in my senior year, when my math teacher told us about a program that would introduce a few highly qualified kids to computers. He said that with my solid performance in calculus, I had a good chance of being selected. I visited the campus again, this time peering at an ugly gray box, about the size of a refrigerator, with a few switches on its front. I hoped to learn everything I could about that box.

While I waited for them to choose the lucky participants, I borrowed a book from the library. Every night I read how computers convert electrical signals into the ones and zeros needed for calculations. I also learned that the world's first computer was developed at the University of Pennsylvania, yet another reason to be proud to live in Philadelphia.

The results finally arrived. A half-dozen students had been selected citywide, my math teacher said, but I wasn't one of them. I couldn't understand this rejection. I deserved to be in this program. I was sick with grief. My math teacher consoled me with the fact that I would still be able to take a free course offered by the university's physics department. So that summer, every day for weeks, I felt a thrill of privilege, attending the class with college students and faculty. The computer instructions resembled algebra equations, except that instead of writing on paper, we punched codes into cards.

My explorations of the city's buildings had, until now, connected me to the past. Learning about computers in the company of all these smart people felt like I was stepping into my future.

After-school Jobs Completed My Education

Most nights Dad was at the drugstore until 10 p.m. On those few nights when the family was together for dinner, he regaled us with stories about customers asking for credit, or giving him a hard time, or buying too much cough syrup with codeine. He talked about the doctor next door coming in an hour late, or about a robbery at a store owned by one of his friends. As I grew older, I realized that if I were ever going to actually be in one of dad's stories, I would need to participate in the family business.

Every weekend that summer, I waited on customers. They asked for cigarettes or placed items from the shelves on the counter. Sometimes they asked for an obscure old remedy and I had to claw through drawers labeled with the letters of the alphabet. My favorite times were when too many prescriptions came in all at once and Dad called me back to help him count out pills.

Sometimes, a child wordlessly handed me a crumpled note. Unable to decipher it, I showed it to my father, who told me which bottle to get. How did he always know? When I handed it to the little boy I recognized a glimmer of pride on his face. He had fulfilled his parent's mission as I was fulfilling mine.

One day, a young man came into the drugstore and asked, "Is Doc in?" Based on the stethoscope around his neck, I guessed he was one of the medical school students who lived in the dormitory across the street.

I went into the back. "Hey Dad. There's a guy here to see you."

After they greeted each other, Dad pointed to me. "You've already met my son, Jerry." I heard an unfamiliar hint of pride. *Was he showing me off?*

The man, Dr. Lewis, looked at me. "I hear you're interested in becoming a doctor. If you would like to visit me at the hospital, I'll show you what I do."

The following week, I stopped at the hospital's emergency room and asked for Dr. Lewis. He greeted me and ushered me behind a curtain where he had been examining a roundish, balding man who sat with his shirt off. Picking up his examination from where he had left off, Dr. Lewis pointed to a wide-mouthed glass bottle filled almost to the brim with urine.

"Judging from the size of that urine sample," he said to the patient, "I'd say you've been drinking. That might explain why you aren't feeling well."

The man nodded in agreement. "Yes, doc, I have been drinking, but that's not it. I've been feeling so run down lately."

Doctor Lewis turned to me. "We see so many alcoholics in here. Look at his hairless chest. In advanced stages, alcoholics exhibit feminine traits because the liver is so damaged it can no longer break down female hormones."

At first I was self-conscious that he was speaking to me as if I was on the staff. Then I shifted my perspective and imagined Dr. Lewis speaking to me as a colleague. This was a glimpse of what it could feel like in a few years if I continued on my present course.

I walked the three blocks from the hospital to Dad's store, giddy with anticipation of my future career.

Dad must have noticed my excitement because a few weeks later he told me he had good news.

"I talked to my friend Bernie, who owns the drugstore next to the medical school. Bernie said one of the doctors who eats at his lunch counter could give you a part-time job."

When I went to the pharmacology research center to meet my potential boss, a sandy-haired man with a gentle smile came out to greet me. "Hi, I'm Dr. Rusy. Sorry about the outfit." He gestured to his flimsy green pajama-like clothes. "When I'm not here doing research, I work in the hospital as an anesthesiologist."

His lab was filled with a trove of interesting equipment, like oscilloscopes and other electronic devices strung together with wires.

Gesturing to a stainless-steel operating table, he said, "We study how drugs affect the volume of blood flowing through the heart. To gather data, we implant a device near a dog's aorta. Your job is to wash the glassware after these experiments."

We walked across the hall to the sink, where a pile of beakers and test tubes sat in a tub of sudsy water.

"What is that?" I pointed to the red sludge at the bottom of many of the test tubes.

"We spin blood samples in a centrifuge and measure the solids that fall to the bottom. That is called the hematocrit."

"Hematocrit," I repeated. I was already learning about the composition of blood. I couldn't believe my good fortune. This was exactly where I wanted to be.

Every day after school, I took the subway to Broad and Erie, walked to the lab, and washed glassware. Then, with time to kill, I asked Dr. Rusy about his research. He told me if I wanted to get the whole story, I could take books out of the medical library and he would be happy to answer any questions.

I went downstairs to the library in the older part of the building, so quiet and somber it seemed holy. I imagined a hundred years of medical students scanning these shelves and studying for exams at these tables. I flipped through a book on physiology, awed by the knowledge I held in my hands. Back in Dr. Rusy's lab I scanned the chapters, greedily absorbing information about various bodily systems.

I was especially attracted to the simplicity and power of the heart, whose chambers squeezed blood in a perfectly orchestrated sequence. The signals for this sequence were transmitted by specialized nerve cells called *Purkinje Fibers*. I rolled the sound on my tongue. Per … Kin … Jee. …

I jumped to another chapter about how blood picks up oxygen from the lungs and carries it through the body, where it drops off the oxygen in exchange for carbon dioxide. When I had my fill of gas exchanges, I leapt to the way the kidneys filtered waste matter out of the blood through an intricate network of tubules. To my delight, the tubules had another wonderful name— *glomeruli*. I savored each syllable. Glom … err … you … lie. It sounded like music.

Reading these books in the lab felt the same as when I was standing at the candy counter at my dad's store, eating as much as I wanted. Unlike chocolate bars, though, these facts tasted as sweet after the hundredth one as they did after the first.

Something to Believe In

Out of all the boys in the honors class, Arthur was the one with whom I could most easily share my passion for knowledge. The one time when I visited his house in the northeast of the city, we pored through the issue of *Scientific American* with a beautiful cover photo of the double helix, the genetic code of life. Each amino acid – guanine, adenine, thymine, and cytosine – rolled off our lips like a magical incantation, summoning forth our power over nature.

Despite these moments of perfect harmony, Arthur and I seemed to be drifting apart in another way. While my interest in Judaism waned, Arthur's had increased. He had even begun wearing a small knitted skullcap to school. We never discussed our differences, but I sometimes wondered why he was so intense about religion.

Before the summer break of our senior year, he told me he was going to Israel with his Jewish youth group. I understood the importance of Israel in our history. Every year at Passover, when we commemorated the liberation of Jews from slavery in Egypt, I felt goosebumps of pride. However, that holiday celebrated events that took place thousands of years ago. When my grandparents fled persecution in Russia, they landed in the United States. I needed to find my identity in this time and place.

Through the summer, I again worked at my dad's drugstore, and went on my pilgrimages into Center City. When Arthur returned, I phoned to welcome him back. I sat alone in my kitchen at the booth, glad to hear a friendly voice.

He told me how important Israel had been to him and how, by feeling the soil beneath his feet, he felt closer to his Jewish heritage than ever before. Then he asked me, "Would you ever go to Israel?" His voice sounded edgy, as if he were seeking more than a simple answer.

"I don't know. Maybe."

"You know what your problem is? You don't believe in anything." Now he sounded blatantly sarcastic, like he was speaking down to me. *What did I do wrong?*

"That's not true," I said, sinking lower in the booth.

"OK. So what *do* you believe in?"

I stammered, not sure what he was getting at.

He bellowed, "What would you die for?"

"I don't know," I said again, horrified at what he was asking me to consider. He was my only friend. I didn't want to offend him. Die for? I loved ideas, but the notion of boiling down my entire reason to live to one single purpose seemed impossible.

Finally I squeaked out, "I never thought about it. Probably nothing." I couldn't believe he had pushed the conversation this far.

"You're useless," he said in disgust. I started to cry, and he hung up, leaving me shaken and bewildered by his intensity.

What would I die for? Arthur's accusation had the sting of truth. I didn't really know.

§§§

Twelfth-grade physics was my favorite subject. The teacher, Mr. Hofkin, was tall and handsome, with carefully coiffed hair and an elegant, generous manner. He smiled a lot and answered questions ferociously, as if by sheer determination he could help me understand everything there was to know about physics.

Physics taught me equations for things I had always taken for granted. Now when I drove my car, I could visualize the mathematics that governed velocity and acceleration. In the second semester, the lessons explained increasingly subtle phenomena. When he told us that electricity, magnetism, and light could all be described by the same set of equations, I just stared in disbelief, delighted that the universe, which seemed so mysterious, might yield its secrets after all.

Quantum mechanics, though, was the ultimate topic. It stretched me beyond the things I could see, to an Alice-in-Wonderland world I could barely imagine. Its paradoxes sounded too crazy to be considered scientific. After class I asked Mr. Hofkin if he could sum up the essence of quantum mechanics. He hesitated, searching for the right words. Then he explained that in experiments, results change depending on the presence or absence of an observer. That defied everything I had learned about science, which had always claimed that truth existed even if no one was watching.

I wondered what my older brother thought about these bizarre scientific principles. Because of the difference in our ages, we never hung out much, except for the summer when he couldn't find work and we sat outside on the porch playing chess for hours every day. Before he went back to college, he showed me how to solder transistors onto a circuit board to help him build a stereo. Now that he was in medical school in New York City, I wanted to relate to him on a more adult level, and my physics course gave me the opportunity. I wrote him a letter describing my sense of awe.

In his return letter, he responded, "Isn't it incredible? The orbit of an electron is a vague cloud of probability. When you look at the matter all around you, it is mostly empty space."

My connection with my brother about the laws of the universe felt so grown up and important. I wanted this feeling to last for the rest of my life. I asked Dr. Rusy if studying physics in college would be a good qualification for admission to medical school. He said that his own undergraduate degree had been in Electrical Engineering, and any major in hard sciences would put me in a strong position.

I had charted my path. By continuing to study math and physics, I would become an expert in the sublime truths of science. These would lead me toward medical school. Medical school was my Promised Land. I doubted my passion for knowledge rose to Arthur's high standard: I didn't think I would die for it. But my desire to learn as much as possible was beginning to feel as important as life itself.

Understanding My Own Mind

I completed high school in January, the last time Philadelphia's schools would have a mid-year graduating class. The fact that I would be out of school for eight months both exhilarated and scared me. I was like a soldier who had been forced onto the battlefield without complete training. Fortunately, this particular battlefield was easy. My boss at the medical research lab hired me to work fulltime, doing little more than I had done for him before.

To enhance my status as a workingman, I accompanied my father every morning—two men on their way to work. His destination was the drugstore where he was going to sell drugs. Mine was the pharmacology department to research how drugs operate.

Since I worked at the lab all day, I was present when Dr. Rusy performed surgery on dogs, implanting a device around the aorta that would measure blood flow to the heart. Doctors from the whole department came to watch or even participate. One regular guest was Roger Sevy, the Dean of Admissions at the medical school. When he said hello to me, I felt myself drawing rapidly closer to my goal of becoming a doctor.

During the operation, I watched and listened, trying to learn everything I could from their conversations. After everyone left and my boss returned to his office, I stood at his door. "Could you explain what kind of information you get from all those squiggles on the electrocardiogram?"

He stopped what he was doing and in simple, direct language explained the meaning of the spiky line. His patience made the learning process enjoyable. To make better sense of his explanation, I borrowed a cardiology textbook that helped me match the electrocardiogram's peaks and valleys with the pumping cycle of the heart.

I paid especially close attention to the two parts of the nervous system. One part, the sympathetic system, speeds up the heart in order to give us the extra energy we need during emergencies, and the other part, the parasympathetic system, slows it down when we're calm. This information made me think that my parasympathetic nerves must not be working very well. I seemed to be in a constant state of tension, always worried about who I was supposed to be and what I was supposed to do next. I wondered if there was a way to stimulate my parasympathetic nervous system so I could relax.

To learn more I signed up for freshman psychology, offered at night at Temple University. I was excited to attend my first college class, but the lectures were not about how to understand myself. Instead, they taught things like training dogs to salivate or training pigeons to peck at various levers.

My textbook mentioned Sigmund Freud, the founder of psychiatry, who happened to be Jewish. He wrote from the cauldron of Europe a few decades before the Holocaust. On one of my forays into Center City, I picked up Freud's book, *Civilization and Its Discontents*.

Freud said the human mind consisted of three parts. The *id* pressed us to obey our instincts. The *superego* tried to enforce rules that would keep our instincts in check. The *ego*, sandwiched between the other two, gave us our conscious experience of personhood. These three parts were in constant battle, vying for control.

His description of my inner life scared me. How could I ever feel peaceful if the parts of my mind were in conflict? His explanation also painted a gloomy picture about society. Since we are all at war within ourselves, naturally we erupt into war with each other.

One morning I woke up remembering a dream about my father. Why was my father in my dream? Freud taught that children have sexual urges toward their opposite-sex parents and murderous urges toward their same-sex parent. I feared something was wrong with me.

I approached one of the researchers at the lab, Dr. Herbert Needleman, who always gave me a warm hello. He was a psychiatrist who studied the effects of lead toxicity on inner-city kids. I steeled my courage, went to his office, and asked him if he had a few minutes. He said "sure" and I sat in the chair next to his desk.

"I woke up remembering being in the drugstore with my father."

He sat quietly. I looked at him, waiting for his comment. Finally he said, "That's it? That's what you wanted to talk about?"

"Yes, that, and I'm anxious a lot," I said. "I don't know what's wrong with me."

He leaned back in his chair and smiled. "Relax," he said. "Take it easy. Go out more. You're worrying too much."

But I couldn't take it easy. Life felt so uneasy and out of control. Learning medicine was the only bright spot and I wanted to immerse myself in it. I couldn't wait to begin college . . . but which one?

Decision Day

When the results of the Merit Scholarship tests came in, I had been counted as a semi-finalist, a prestigious award that resulted in a mention in the local newspaper. In that article, I learned that Central had one of the largest number of Merit semi-finalists of any public school in the country.

I wasn't at the top of my class, so I knew I couldn't get into Harvard, Princeton, or Yale, but based on my test scores, and coming from the honors class of such an amazing school, I felt smart enough and prepared enough to attend almost any college I wanted. I ended up applying to seven colleges, including Columbia, Johns Hopkins, Cornell, and of course, the University of Pennsylvania. Of those, the only one that invited me for an interview was Cornell University.

The Greyhound bus arrived in Ithaca, New York at night, the snow and cold so penetrating it took me until morning to shake off the sense of desolation. At the interview, even though the room felt overheated and stuffy, I couldn't get the chill out of my bones.

The interviewer asked me why I wanted to attend this particular school. *Um, because I'm a high school student, and I want to attend a good college?* His stupid question confused me so much, I only nodded and mumbled for the rest of the interview. I couldn't wait to get out of there. Afterward, I was riddled by misgivings. Why couldn't I have told him about Dad's drugstore, or the medical research lab, or my passion for physics and medicine, or that I couldn't wait to be a doctor? Rather than boosting my application, I suspected my performance had ruined it. The whole visit felt so dismal.

It looked like my best chance was the University of Pennsylvania. It was just a subway ride away, it was highly competitive, and it had a great physics department. Best of all, I had heard a rumor that they annually admitted 50 students from Central. Since I was in the honors class, I assumed I would be one of them.

The morning of Decision Day, April 15, 1965, I waited at home alone, playing out every possible scenario about which schools would accept me and which I would attend. Around noon, I heard the flap on the mail slot open and ding shut. In a state of nervous anticipation, I picked the pile off the floor and took it back to the sofa.

Rifling through, I picked out the seven letters. They were all thin. I gulped hard. I'd heard that rejections come in thin envelopes. This couldn't be happening. I opened the first one and quickly saw they had declined my application. Oh, no. As if in a trance, I opened each one, confirming the worst. I saved the University of Pennsylvania for last—but it too was a rejection.

This was the one scenario I had never imagined.

Instead of sitting here selecting which one of the schools to attend, I was sitting here with no future. It was over. All the competitive schools would be closed to applications. What should have been the most exciting day of my life turned into the darkest. Despite the pressure in my eyes, no tears flowed.

When my parents came home, I broke the news. They were shaken, too, and didn't know what to say. Dad suggested I go to Temple. It was in North Philadelphia, a few stops further down the same subway line that I rode to the drugstore. "It would be so convenient," he said. But I had built up a complicated matrix in my mind about what schools would be appropriate and Temple wasn't on the list.

"But you want to go to Temple Medical School," Dad pointed out. "You love it there."

"That's the medical school, Dad. Temple's undergraduate school isn't hard enough."

He looked disappointed. I didn't know how to explain my reluctance, but in my heart I knew that if I didn't attend a competitive school, I would cease to exist.

A few days later, Dad took me to meet a pharmacist in South Philadelphia who was a city councilman and had influence in local politics. We drove to a part of town I had never visited before, through narrow streets. We knocked at the door of the closed drugstore and a heavyset, balding man emerged from the shadows and let us in. Dad seemed as nervous as I was and handed him my scores and grades. The man shook his head. "Maybe if you had asked me before you were rejected, I could have done something. But I'm sorry. There's nothing I can do for you now."

We drove home in silence.

In a panic, I asked everyone I knew for advice. One guy told me his older brother, Larry, attended the University of Wisconsin. That seemed like a crazy idea. Wisconsin was a thousand miles away, and it was a state-sponsored school, which meant it wouldn't be as competitive as the other schools on my list. I hated that, but I didn't know what else to do.

I called Larry and asked him if he thought I should go. "It has a good reputation," he said. "You'll like it."

When I received a catalog, I was relieved to see it had a sizable physics section. When I told my boss at the research center, about my situation, he said, "University of Wisconsin is where I went! It's a great school."

Dr. Rusy had been a wonderful mentor. If it was good enough for him, it would be good enough for me. So I applied. They wrote back to say that they were trying to boost the attendance of their early summer session and they admitted me on the condition that I start in June. That was just a few weeks away. I didn't have time to worry about whether it was the right choice. For now, it was the only choice.

Uprooted

In June of 1965, just two months after the collapse of all my dreams, I was on an airplane for the first time in my life. Larry flew with me as far as Chicago, where he was going to visit his girlfriend. I flew the last leg of the trip alone. Since the dorms wouldn't open until the following day, Larry had given me the key to his apartment.

The taxi dropped me off a few blocks from the campus on a street lined with shops—a record store, a clothing store, a burger joint. Next to each business was a door. I assumed his apartment would be through one of those doors. But the address Larry had written didn't match any of the buildings. I walked the length of the street, peering at the names on the mailboxes, but that didn't help, either.

It was Sunday so most of the stores were closed. Since the main summer session had not yet started, the streets were almost deserted. I was like a ghost in a ghost town, not knowing where I was or where I was going.

Becoming desperate, I walked up to the second floor of each building and knocked on doors—all were empty. The sun blazed and the air felt muggy. I retraced my steps, trying to open all the doors with the key Larry had given me. Eventually one opened. The tension drained out of me as I sank down on the sofa and looked around. The living room was dumpy, with musty sagging chairs and a dirty carpet. So this is a student apartment. It felt better than being lost on the sidewalk.

The next day I carried my suitcase four blocks to Ogg Hall, a tower rising from an open concrete courtyard. Only a few people were in sight. I rode the elevator to the eighth floor and looked around for someone in charge. A pleasant man, a few years older than me, told me he was the resident advisor.

He showed me to my room, just large enough to fit two beds and two desks, separated by a narrow aisle. "Because there are so few students here in the summer, you'll have the room to yourself."

He took me around and introduced me to a half dozen other students on the floor. The guy directly across from me, Nate, was about the same height as me, a little more than six feet, with dark wavy hair and a friendly smile. I took to Nate instantly.

As soon as I unpacked I went back across the hall. "Where are you going to eat lunch?" I asked.

"I don't know. We can find a place."

At a drugstore lunch counter a couple of blocks away, Nate told me he grew up in northwest Wisconsin, near the border of Minnesota and Canada. His town, Superior, was across the river from where Bob Dylan was born. It sounded isolated and cold. Nate's father was an Orthodox Rabbi who had survived the Holocaust.

How odd that my first friend in Madison was more Jewish than anyone I knew at home. Even though my sense of religion no longer connected me with God, I loved the comfort and connection our shared Jewishness gave us. We bonded as if we had known each other for years and spent the summer forming a tight friendship in what was to me, a foreign land.

Occasionally, girls from another wing of the dorm came around for social activities. Except for my disastrous attempts at dates in high school, this was my first exposure to the opposite sex since eighth grade. Some of the boys knew how to banter with them and I tried to learn by watching them.

There was a girl in the crowd with an Italian accent and a delightful name, Sylvia Baraldini. When she learned that I was from Philadelphia she became misty eyed. "Oh you are so lucky to live in a city that has Eugene Ormandy. He is one of my favorite orchestra conductors." Her compliment gave me an unexpected thrill. When I had attended rehearsals at the Academy of Music, I had no idea that the conductor was known around the world.

Another girl, Maggie, was petite and pretty, but she seemed awkward around people and looked upset when one of the boys teased her. I always assumed that pretty girls were in command of every crowd and was surprised to discover that her beauty did not automatically provide her with social graces.

I was taking Calculus II, having skipped the first semester thanks to my advanced placement score. I studied hard, did all my homework, and easily earned A's on my tests. I soon discovered, however, that not all the habits I had formed in my high school honors class were appropriate in my new home.

One day, when Nate and I were talking, he suddenly stopped speaking. He looked angry. I asked him what was wrong. Through clenched teeth he said, "When you say 'obviously,' you seem so arrogant, as if you want me to feel inferior."

"I'm sorry," I stammered. "I didn't even know I was doing it."

We patched it up and I vowed to stop saying 'obviously,' wondering if there was anything else I might be doing that sounded arrogant.

When I told Nate about my classes, I mentioned that in addition to second semester calculus, I was signed up for the second semester of sociology.

"Why the second? You're a freshman." He sounded tense again.

"I didn't want to waste my time, learning all those introductory theories," I said, figuring he would be impressed.

Instead of being impressed, he said, "You see? That's exactly what I'm talking about. You're so arrogant."

"I just like to challenge myself," I said, but he shook his head.

"You're hopeless."

His comment reminded me that it was going to be hard to keep myself engaged with the same intensity here as I maintained in high school. Back then, our hallway quizzes kept me under constant pressure to be my best. Nate's criticism seemed to be heading in the opposite direction. Here, I was going to be criticized for looking smart. My fears about attending a less competitive school were already coming true. If trying to look smart were a bad thing, how would I maintain my motivation?

§§§

As it happened, my reason for taking Sociology 102 was not to impress anyone, or even because it was hard. I hoped the course, called "Social Disorganization," would answer my questions about why humans have such a hard time getting along. Instead, the course only heightened my concerns. In particular, I was disturbed by the concept of "anomie." This term meant that when people lose their interest in social values, they have no more reason to obey the rules.

To illustrate the idea of anomie, the professor wheeled in a record player and played a haunting song called *Pirate Jenny*, sung by Nina Simone. The song told the story of a cleaning woman on her knees, scrubbing the floor, while everyone walked past, barely noticing her.

She imagined a pirate ship coming into the harbor and blasting the town with its cannons. The pirates captured the fine, upstanding citizens of the town, threw them down in front of Jenny, and asked her, "Should we kill them now or later?" She said, "Right now."

There it was again, the inner war of individuals creating the mayhem of society. Humans seemed determined to tear apart the world. Perhaps someday I would understand it better. For now, I wanted to forget the creepy image of a cleaning maid destroying society with her hatred. To lift my spirits, I walked around the campus, admiring the way humans kept building things up.

Bascom Hall, with its tall columns and arches, stood majestically at the top of a steep tree-lined hill. In front of the building sat the statue of Abe Lincoln, whose furrowed brow reminded me of the effort required to keep society together in the face of strife.

The area immediately around this hill was landscaped in grass and trees, and beautifully crafted buildings. Past Bascom Hall, an old carillon tower transported me to a simpler, more majestic time. Farther still, buildings sprawled in a variety of styles, from old red brick ones to modern concrete and glass.

When I walked among them, I felt a thrill of history, as though I could see the past hundred years all laid out and coming alive before me. Feeling the history of this place also helped me feel grounded, connected with my new home.

As the angry echoes of Pirate Jenny faded from my mind, I felt more relaxed. I breathed in the gentle breeze and headed over to the Student Union, intending to sit on the terrace and watch the sun sparkle on the lake. I turned the corner and found myself in a small crowd. They were watching a few people walking in a circle, holding picket signs.

I asked someone in the crowd what was going on. He said, "They're protesting the war in Vietnam." I had never heard of the war in Vietnam, and had never seen a picket line in person. *Who are these people? What is Vietnam?*

Looking for My Groove

In September, 30,000 students descended on Madison so fast I felt as though I had stepped into a raging river. The high-rise dorms transformed into a swarming maze, and like a child thrown into the water, I had to learn how to swim.

My roommate, Bob, a journalism major from Milwaukee, should have been a natural ally. But after a few awkward stabs at conversation we discovered we had almost nothing to say to each other.

Most of the other boys on my floor were freshmen, away from home for the first time. Since we all shared a bathroom, I quickly knew everyone at least enough to say hello.

The boys were from cultures that I had never known, Swedes and Norwegians, with high cheekbones, small noses and straight hair, some raised on farms in rural towns. One guy proudly told me that Wisconsin makes the best cheese. After a visit home, he brought back a huge block of cheddar that was manufactured in his hometown. After tasting it, I had to agree. It was delicious.

Just getting to know them by name was not helping me figure out how to relate. The differences between my dorm-mates and myself were most apparent Friday and Saturday nights. After studying at the library, I was usually in bed by 10 p.m. Then frequently, I was awakened at 2 a.m. by shouting—the drunks were back from the bar. I'd wake up, angry for being disturbed and disgusted at their sloppy, raucous behavior. I had never been to a bar and didn't understand this weekend ritual. I'd roll over and eventually fall back to sleep.

One Saturday night, I was startled awake by a strange sensation. It took me a moment to realize my bed was shaking, a seemingly impossible event on a high floor of a concrete and steel structure. Staggering into the hallway, I followed the sound of screaming and laughing to a dormitory room, packed with a dozen guys. By then the shaking stopped and I asked one of them what was going on.

"We were conducting an experiment," he said. "Mike learned in engineering class that a group of soldiers marching across a bridge could set the whole thing into harmonic motion. We wanted to see if we could shake the whole dorm so we were jumping up and down in unison." By adjusting their timing to match the vibration frequency of the building, each jump reinforced the wave before, resulting in ever-increasing ripples through the concrete. Fortunately, they got tired – or scared – of their game before we ended in rubble.

Mixed in with my anger about their wildness, I felt a tinge of jealousy. They had turned an engineering lesson into an opportunity to have fun, to laugh and talk and experiment. By contrast, I left my physics class feeling alone. I had never really figured out how to talk with fellow students about those subjects, and as a result did not know a single person in my physics class.

My companionship with Nate, which felt so easy in the calm of the summer, seemed out of step with the frantic pace of the fall. After a few weeks of random connections, I became friendly with a couple of Jewish guys from the suburbs of New York. I always thought of New York as the center of all culture, and I wanted to spend as much time as possible with each of them, trying to make sense of the world through their eyes.

One of them, Mark, turned me on to a comedy recording called the *Two Thousand Year Old Man*, by Mel Brooks and Carl Reiner. One track of the record was an interview with a flaky psychiatrist who said he was "Docker Haldanish," rather than "Doctor."

The interviewer asked, "Have you ever cured anyone?"

"Yes," Docker Haldanish replied.

"What was wrong with her?"

Docker Haldanish replied, very drily, "She was tearing paper."

"How did you cure her?"

"I said, 'Don't tear paper.'"

Mark and I cracked up every time we heard this routine. We listened to the gags over and over, until they became part of our conversation. When one of us was frustrated with some situation, the other would shift into interviewer mode and ask, "How would you stop it?" The answer was always "Don't tear paper," attempting to imitate Mel Brooks's New York accent, after which we would dissolve into laughter.

Despite Mark's enjoyment of a good laugh, he hated being in Madison, and he griped routinely about having to be here. He told me once that any day he spent outside of New York was a day wasted. I knew all about his wish to be at a better school, but I was in Madison now and trying to make the most of it.

My other friend, Alex, was from Larchmont, New York, the same suburb as Mark. Instead of worrying about being in Madison, Alex worried about being in the world. All three of us shared some secret anxiety: Even though we rarely talked about being Jewish, we all knew the world could turn against us, violently, at any moment.

Whereas Mark broke the tension with laughter, Alex broke it with pot. When he offered me some, I didn't know what he was talking about. I didn't even know such a thing existed. "Just try it. It's very hip." We smoked together, and the first time all I got was a headache. I wanted to understand more about it, so I kept trying.

After a few times, the headaches transformed into strange new sensations. I felt detached from the world, enabling me to see everything in a zany, offbeat way. Everyone's jokes were funnier, and my thoughts, which were intense to begin with, became even more interesting. And best of all, when I smoked marijuana, I felt like I belonged to some secret insider club.

Alex's other contribution to my life was music. He worked as a clerk at the record store on State Street, near where I stayed the first night I was in Madison. I regularly stopped in to see him on my way back from class. He introduced me to the other employees, most of whom were jazz musicians. The guys who worked at the shop were clearly part of the club I wanted to get into, and to earn their respect, I hung around and asked them questions about the latest albums.

My favorite spot in the store was in front of the New Releases rack. Each new record promised a new way of looking at the world. I picked up each album, by artists like the Beatles, the Rolling Stones, Bob Dylan, and Otis Redding, stared at the pictures, and read everything on the front and back. Sometimes they contained the lyrics, which I read carefully. I often talked to the staff to get their opinions about the new albums. My record collection began to grow, with rock and roll, folk rock, and soul. One day, Alex pointed to the fine print on the back of an Aretha Franklin album. It said the producer was Jerry Waxler. He laughed and said it was a typo. The producer's real name was

Jerry Wexler, and he was famous for discovering many successful musicians.

My interest in music made me want to hang around with musicians, so when I heard another freshman, Paul, playing a guitar at a meeting room in the dorm, I introduced myself. He was from a small town near Washington, D.C. Even though he wasn't Jewish, his good looks, charm, and passion for music intrigued me. We chatted a few times, and whenever he played in the meeting room, I made it a point to be there. One day, he told me he was starting a band and asked me if I wanted to join. I laughed nervously.

"How is that possible? I don't play an instrument."

"It's easy to learn how to play the bass guitar. I'll show you the chords. C'mon. It will be fun."

It was hard to picture myself making music, but if he thought I could do it, maybe I could. And it would open up a whole new type of social interaction. I could hang out with the musicians and perhaps girls would look at me differently. We made plans to get started right after spring break. When I flew home, I felt a combination of fear and nervous anticipation about this new venture.

When I returned, I wasn't in my dorm room for more than a few minutes when the residential advisor knocked on my door.

"I know you were close to Paul. I've got some bad news. He was killed in a car crash."

"What? How?"

"I heard that he was high on LSD. He drove through a red light and was broadsided in the intersection."

I couldn't imagine Paul gone, and just as important, I couldn't believe my opportunity to make music had been ripped away from me before it even started. With a lump in my throat, I jumped up and ran to the stairwell, racing up the stairs, trying to think. How could this happen? How could people die? Why him? Why now? When I reached the top of the high-rise I ran down the stairs two at a time, and then at the ground floor, gasping for air, I started up again, until I was exhausted. I was unable to answer any of my questions.

The only place I could reliably count on answers was in my physics course. I understood why Sir Isaac Newton was viewed as a god in his own time. By inventing calculus, he had given the world a language to explain the mysteries of gravity and acceleration. I didn't worship the man, but I worshipped the purity and simplicity of his explanations. These clean, consistently solvable problems satisfied my need for a world that made sense.

Since physics was so satisfying, I wanted to immerse myself in it as much as possible. I discovered that the chairman of the physics department was also in charge of the medical physics department. This sounded like a perfect opportunity to combine my two passions. I made an appointment to ask how I could learn more about this exciting field. He seemed exceptionally friendly and said he could always use part-time help in his lab. I was thrilled.

The actual work turned out to be less exciting than I hoped. My job was to grind pieces of irradiated bone. This was a cruel twist of fate. In Dad's drugstore, I crushed pills and powders in a mortar and pestle. Now, I was using the same equipment to grind bones. Crushing baked animal bones into dust was not only repetitive, but made my stomach churn. After a few sessions, I told my boss I was having second thoughts and maybe I wouldn't be able to fit part-time work into my schedule after all.

My bone-grinding job was a symptom of a bigger problem. Physics classes didn't help me relate to people. From the end of one session to the start of the next, I never spoke a word about science or math. It was a lonely feeling and I was tired of being lonely.

A solution to my isolation began to emerge from the Vietnam War protests. Regular presenters in the meeting room argued that the U.S. government had trumped up this conflict in order to test weapons and exercise military might. After the heated meetings, we talked for hours about how the war was unnecessary and that together we were going to stop it.

By the spring, indoor meetings escalated into outdoor rallies. One day, a crowd of students gathered outside the administration building, and the organizer shouted through a bullhorn: We were going to take over the building. I wasn't sure how this would help, but I had to do something.

That evening, just before the building was supposed to close, around a hundred of us entered and simply refused to leave. The police didn't make a fuss. They let us have our way. I sat on the floor of the linoleum-tiled hallway, leaning against the wall, observing the conversations around me.

One of the protestors, Ron, smiled and chatted with everyone who came close, as if he was everyone's friend, including mine. Through the course of the long night, his surprisingly open manner reached a peak when he turned to a pretty blond girl next to him and said. "You've got great legs." When he reached out to touch her, his easy familiarity with her shocked me. But she didn't seem to mind. She even smiled.

When she left, I introduced myself to Ron and told him how impressed I was by his brash behavior. He smiled and said he couldn't help it. "Those legs were calling to me, man."

Hoping to learn how to be more like him, I struck up a conversation. When he told me he lived in an apartment off campus, I was surprised.

"Isn't there a rule that says all freshmen have to live in dorms?" I asked.

He smirked as if to say, *Those rules have nothing to do with me.*

The night turned into dawn and as we were preparing to leave, another girl said, "Hi." She wasn't talking to Ron. She was talking to me. She had light brown, almost blond hair, an aquiline nose and big, pretty eyes. What struck me most was her friendliness.

I assumed girls would only speak to me if I spoke first. Since I never had the nerve to say anything, this usually meant I didn't speak to girls. For some reason, she was breaking the rules. I wondered if some of Ron's charisma had rubbed off on me.

Trying to act naturally, I said, "Hi." If she sensed my awkwardness, it didn't seem to bother her.

We talked about the protest, and I told her I was from Philadelphia. She said she grew up in Madison. Her father was a psychology professor. She asked if we could go out sometime. I said "Sure," and told her I would call her. Inside, I was in a panic. I had no idea what I was supposed to do. I found Ron to ask him for his advice.

"This could be the big one, man," he said. "Why don't you use my apartment?"

"Are you sure?" I asked, grateful for the offer.

"No problem, man. I'll do something else for the night."

"I've never done anything like this," I said. "I'm not sure what to do."

"You'll figure it out," he said with a laugh.

I called her the next day and arranged a meeting. That weekend, I walked to her dorm near campus. When she came out to the lobby to meet me, I told her we were going to a friend's apartment. She immediately jumped into the plan.

"OK," she said. "And it doesn't matter what time we get back. If the doors are locked, I can just climb in the window." I couldn't believe how open she was about defying the rules. She must have done this before.

On the walk to Ron's place, I grew increasingly nervous. It was chilly and I started to tremble. The closer we got, the harder I shook, until finally I sat down on the curb, hoping to regain my composure.

"Are you OK?"

"Yes," I said, casting my gaze down. I didn't feel OK.

After a few minutes, I stood up and we continued walking, but I was hardly able to speak. Once inside, we sat next to each other on a sofa, alone in candlelight, but my nerves were so taut I couldn't even bring myself to hold her hand. After an awkward silence that seemed to last forever, we walked back to her place, and she said goodnight. She smiled as if to say she understood and then climbed over the wall. I slunk back to my dorm, devastated by my failure. If I couldn't even make it with a willing girl, how would I ever break through my loneliness?

Knowledge Was My Friend

To ease my fears of being alone, I returned to my books with a vengeance. Each new section in the physics book offered another revelation about the world, making me feel like, at least in this one area, my life was on the right track. Geniuses like Isaac Newton described equations for the attraction of gravity and the force of acceleration. And James Clerk Maxwell discovered that electricity, light, magnetism, and radio waves were different forms of one phenomenon. The fact that so many systems could be described by mathematical equations reinforced my greatest hope: That by learning science, I would soon be able to understand everything in the universe. Since I first fell in love with physics in high school, this hope had alleviated the anxiety that seemed to constantly hover around me like a cloud.

Schoolwork came easy, and my grades qualified me for the national freshman honors society. To improve my qualifications for medical school, I wrote to Dr. Rusy at the pharmacology department at Temple University and asked him for a job. He arranged a grant that would pay me to conduct my own experiment.

I moved back into my room in Philadelphia and went to the research lab to get started. Dr. Rusy explained my job for the summer. I had to answer a specific question: How are drugs metabolized in various parts of the body?

"After you administer any drug," he explained, "it is absorbed into the various tissues. For example, if you take an aspirin, it first goes into the gut, then is absorbed into the blood. Drugs also can be absorbed into muscle and fat."

The simple equations that would describe the movement of the drug from one body compartment to another were identical to the ones I studied throughout freshman physics, providing more evidence that math could explain everything.

"That's the whole project?" I asked. "It seems so easy."

Dr. Rusy seemed pleased at my complaint. "I know it doesn't seem like much, but applying mathematical models to the study of pharmaceuticals is a hot topic. In fact, we just hired a mathematician last year to help us develop these types of experiments."

"But what is there to do? It's basically just one equation." I was puzzled about how this would keep me busy all summer.

"Well, you have to learn the equipment. And you can dig around through the literature and try to find other research papers that are doing similar things."

Dr. Rusy was trained as an electrical engineer, and I could sense his pleasure when he showed me the lab equipment. With his help, I graphed the way various drugs moved through the body. The real power of the project came from his analog computer, which was a cabinet of neat little rectangular panels with tiny dials, and holes into which you patched in wires. I loved playing with this thing. All I had to do was insert the wires, turn the dials, and the electronics would do the rest.

Now that I was a researcher, I felt even more comfortable around the other doctors in the department and started to feel like I belonged there. We often ate lunch together at the cafeteria. They spoke to me respectfully and I tried to hang around and learn whatever I could about their research.

Since I didn't have any friends left in Philadelphia, I went to work at my dad's drugstore on weekends. Compared with the hectic crowded college campus, living here felt even lonelier than I remembered.

By the end of the summer, I was able to electronically generate the graphs I would use in my report. The curves looked similar to ones I had seen in my math and physics books, but rather than the trajectory of a ball, or the graph of an abstract equation, these showed the concentration of drugs in the gut, blood, fat, and muscle.

I presented my findings to all the doctors in the department, and when I was finished, they applauded, some of them even getting to their feet, and exclaiming "Well done!" and "Really good work!" I was sure the congratulations and admiring comments from a room full of doctors would help in three years when I was ready to go to medical school.

But something about the project bothered me. I had just won all this praise for a few simple calculus equations that generated a few simple graphs. I looked around at these prestigious men and women in their lab coats. Dr. Rusy was there, and even Dr. Sevy, the chairman of the admissions department. I was in the center of the dream, but instead of bliss, I felt a dark shudder of doubt. *Do I really want to pursue this goal?*

In a week, I would be back in Madison, among those masses of students, and whatever I did in this room wasn't going to help me there. I was going to have to figure out how to navigate through the crowds, how to meet girls, and how to stop the war. I looked around the room again. These people had no idea what was going on. Being a doctor seemed like a dream that had little to do with the challenges ahead.

More Attempts to Fit In

In the fall, my parents drove me to the airport for the beginning of my second year away. I felt glad to be leaving Philadelphia. Perhaps this year I would meet a girl. I hoped that moving into an apartment would increase my chances.

My two roommates and I quickly negotiated which room belonged to whom. I wanted the small one in the back, not much bigger than the bed and desk it contained. As we arranged our rooms, Mark continued griping about being in Madison. His summer in New York with his intellectual friends reinforced his desire to be back east. My other roommate, also from New York, had made many friends in Madison and as soon as his room was set up, he went to hang out with them. Soon I was back out to the streets, walking around campus and trying to acclimate myself to being around so many students.

The bookstore was so crowded I had to jostle sideways just to navigate through the aisles, using the stacks of books to help me decide which courses to take. I recognized that my obsession with mathematics and science had left me ignorant of some of the topics that kept coming up in the anti-war movement, so I decided to take classes on the foundations of civilization.

After making my decisions, I went to complete my registration in a huge hall, with dozens of long lines of students all buzzing and waiting. I looked around at the Wisconsinites. I felt like such an outsider.

As evening approached on my way back to the apartment, I realized how different my life would be this year. No more dormitory cafeteria with twenty guys from my floor pushing tables together so we could be close to each other. Now there was no one.

I certainly didn't intend to spend much time in the apartment, with its beat-up furniture, dim lighting, and two disgruntled guys. In the Student Union I heard about a meal plan that served an all-you-can-eat buffet, so I signed up for that. Since I didn't know anyone, I ate by myself, bringing a book with me for company.

When I glanced around the room, one table attracted my attention. Six or eight people gathered every night and I became accustomed to staring at them. A mix of girls and guys, they seemed unusually jovial and I wondered what it was like to have so much company. One day, standing in line at the buffet, one of the guys from the group turned to me and said, "Hi. I'm Devin. I notice you sit alone. You're welcome to join us." He had a deep, friendly voice that made me feel comfortable.

"Thanks. ... I'm Jerry. I'd like that."

I followed him to the table and they all looked up at me and smiled. I wasn't accustomed to people being glad to see me and I was especially surprised to be sitting with girls. However, as they introduced themselves, their good cheer set me at ease.

One was Devin's girlfriend, Ellen. He immediately pointed out the obvious. "Yes, it's true, we're different heights," and everyone laughed at the contrast between his over-six-foot frame and hers, closer to five. A couple of the girls were Ellen's roommates, including a blond, Katy. Even though she was cute, rather than exuding sexuality, she invited friendship, introducing me to the surprising possibility that I might be able to become friends with a girl. From then on, I looked forward to eating with them every evening. Since my own roommates were never home, I occasionally stopped by Devin, Ellen, and Katy's apartment. I was happy to have some people to hang out with.

Throughout the semester, the air hummed with an urgent responsibility to stop the war. A secret dream pervaded our conversations, our posters, and our protests—the vague but exciting idea that if we could stop this war, we might be able to stop all wars. I demonstrated my convictions by growing my hair long and bushy, puffed into a mass of curls, and grew my sideburns out to muttonchops. I limited my clothing to just blue jeans and wrinkled work shirts. Girl protestors didn't wear makeup or do anything fancy with their hair. We hated the superficiality of anyone who didn't obey these rules. We assumed that short-haired guys who ironed their clothes craved power, supported the war, and perpetuated violence.

I couldn't figure out Devin's place in all of this. His hair was long enough, but he dressed a little too neatly. Fortunately he was growing a beard, a comforting sign that confirmed his commitment to the cause. Then one day, he came to dinner with his beard shaved on the right half of his face and completely intact on the left side. I looked at him, puzzled. After much laughter, smirking, and fake philosophical diatribes, he admitted he had done it as a joke. He said it was a protest against the protests. While the rest of the guys on campus were becoming increasingly serious about hair, he had turned it into an opportunity to laugh. A few days later he shaved off the rest of the beard. I began to wonder how serious he was about life.

Shortly after that episode, I started complaining to Devin about how horrific and negative the world is. He didn't agree with me and argued that life is not as bad as I was claiming. I couldn't understand how he could say such a thing. Didn't he see what was going on? European history was filled with the graveyards of man's inhumanity to man. Devin tried to rebuff my cynicism, saying I was painting too dark a picture. The more he tried to convince me the world wasn't so bad, the more forcefully I argued that nothing made sense, nor could it ever.

Finally, in one of our conversations, when I was pushing him hard to agree with my perspective about the cruelty and meaninglessness of life, he pointed out that there is always the existence of God to buffer us from chaos. "There is a sensibility in that higher reality even if we can't always know what it is."

I was disgusted, horrified, and sputtering mad. "You're telling me you believe in God? What kind of argument is that? All God is good for is giving people an excuse to kill each other."

"No, that's religion," Devin said, calmly. "God isn't like that."

"I don't know what you're talking about. I don't know of any God, and I don't think it's appropriate for you to use that in an argument. That's pure irrationality. What's wrong with you?" I was upset now, not just with the world, but more immediately with Devin. "This is stupid."

I stormed off and avoided Devin for weeks. *How could he be so naïve? What a waste of a good mind. There's nothing you can rationally say about the existence of God. The whole concept is a complete distraction.*

I stopped eating dinner with the crowd, and timed my arrival and departure to avoid them. But a few weeks later I grew weary of my self-imposed exile. I dropped by the girls' apartment. Katy had just made a batch of cookies, cooling on the stove, and she offered me one. It was hard not to relax around them. I settled into the plate of cookies, glad to be surrounded by people who seemed to care about me. When Devin came by, he didn't seem upset. He still laughed warmly and seemed eager to be friends.

Listening to them laughing, I realized none of them was Jewish. I wondered what it felt like to grow up without feeling like the world was trying to kill you. I dropped my anger about Devin believing in God. Even though I couldn't understand why a rational person would believe in such a thing, he was a nice guy and I didn't hold it against him.

Just before going home for winter break, Devin introduced me to a friend of his. "You might be interested to know Carl is heading to Italy for a semester abroad."

Carl, like so many Midwesterners, was pleasant and easy to talk to. "Why are you going to Italy?" I asked.

"I love Dante's *Inferno* so much I decided that I needed to read it in its original Italian. When I apply to medical school, I'm going to tell them I'm the president of the *Dante Society*." He laughed and I looked at him, trying to understand the joke. He continued, "I'm the only member of the society," he said, and this time, I laughed with him.

Devin and Carl were similar to me in that they seemed to look at the world as a puzzle. Unlike me, they seemed to have a built-in optimism that they would solve the puzzle. I felt desperately afraid that I wouldn't. Their confidence kept them sane, even though the world was obviously falling apart. *How did they do that?*

As the first semester came to a close, I didn't renew my meal contract at the Student Union. It was expensive and besides, the people who ate there were dressed too well and had short hair. I didn't feel like I belonged there. In fact, I wasn't sure where I belonged.

Culture Wars

The harsh wind of the Wisconsin winter cut into me as I trudged down Bascom Hill to the red brick Armory. Lulled by the rhythm and solitude, propelling my body through the water in the swimming pool there made me feel fit and alive, and let me forget my worries for a half hour every day.

During my brief walk back to the Student Union, the wet hair that poked out of my hat froze into icicles.

Inside the overheated building, the post-exercise euphoria dissipated, as I looked among the crowd for a familiar face. When I nodded to someone I recognized, I felt comforted by the returned greeting. Sadly, not a single one was from my physics classes. All the students in my major were male, and not one of them had made any effort to be my friend. If they were socializing anywhere, I didn't know about it. It certainly wasn't in the Student Union.

I recognized a few students from war protests, or from Alex's musician friends, or from my large art history class. Unlike my physics and math classes, art history teemed with girls.

I loved my art history class. It enabled me to see ancient cultures in new ways, not through wars and political struggles, but through their artistic achievements. We started the year learning about archeological artifacts such as deer painted on the walls of caves, and primitive jewelry placed in graves. Then we progressed to the statues of ancient Greece. Their smooth, almost erotic curves captured the beauty of the human form in stone, carved thousands of years ago. With each new lesson I watched art evolve, from Greece to the magnificent sculpture and architecture of the Roman Empire.

Unlike the silence that followed each math or physics class, we filed out of art history classes chattering about the images and the culture presented during the lecture. Although I was too withdrawn to strike up conversations, I sometimes felt so excited by something we learned in class that I blurted out to whoever happened to be around, "Such beauty!" or "So magical!" When I received a response or even just a smile, for that moment, I felt connected with people through art.

Through all those years in high school, I had never been able to share artistic wonder with my intellectually driven classmates. Art history was opening up another dimension of myself.

I also took a course in European Cultural History in order to understand more about the glories and horrors of the twentieth century. We read novels written by authors from England, France, and Germany. After each one, we attempted to make sense of the culture, based on the stories within each book. Just as the art history course showed history through the eyes of visual art, my cultural history class was teaching me to see history through the eyes of fiction.

Until I took the course, I read novels to immerse myself in the world inside the story. After I took the course, I saw the world outside the novel as an expression of the author's view. Armed with this new angle of vision, I learned to read deeper, losing myself in the story while learning about the world.

§§§

My cultural exploration also expanded my life through jazz. After classes, I often met Alex at the Student Union to listen to his jazz musician-friends jam on the small stage. I rode the waves of the abstract riffs on clarinet, saxophone, drums, and the upright bass. Looking around at the girls sitting nearby, I felt the magnetic pull of their unattainable attractions. My secret hope was that some of the charisma of the music might help me meet people.

One day, Alex introduced me to a girl and said they were a couple. Seeing them together reminded me how far away that possibility was for me. Even talking to a girl seemed remote. I couldn't imagine actually pairing with one.

Karen giggled and whispered in his ear. Alex turned to me and said, "Karen knows someone you might be interested in. Do you want to meet her?"

My heart raced. "Who is she?" I asked, stalling for time.

Karen leaned close and whispered to him again. "Karen thinks you'll like her," he said.

"OK," I said. "If you think she'll go out with me."

So that Saturday evening I walked over to Alex's place and met Sheri. She was tall and cute, which I would have found incredibly intimidating, except she also seemed to be very, very young. She didn't say much and giggled a lot. Her lack of confidence made me feel bolder. The four of us sat together and smoked pot, and then walked to a party. Sheri looped her arm through mine, which was fun.

We could hear blaring music as we approached the apartment. Opening the door, the smell of pot, beer, and bodies signaled we were at the right place. The lights were low, the music loud, and everyone was stoned.

After dancing and mingling and smoking more dope, Sheri and I found an empty bedroom. She seemed dreamy, apparently even more stoned than I was, and we started making out. Soon, our clothes were off, and the last thing I said to her before this major milestone was, "Are you sure you want to do this?" She looked at me with a faraway expression, not registering that I was offering an opportunity to back down. "What?" she said, and I said, "Oh, never mind."

Afterward, we went back to my apartment. We were clinging, hugging and kissing now. I no longer felt intimidated, and her smiles were like big "yes" signs that erased all my fears. We repeated our passionate lovemaking several times, and finally she left.

After all those years of wondering what it was like, I was no longer a virgin. But despite this new status, I was no closer to being part of a couple. I had no idea who Sheri was. I doubt we said more than a few sentences to each other the whole time. My worries about life and school soon closed in on me, and I returned to my routine as if nothing happened.

A few days later Sheri tapped me on the shoulder. I was studying in the library and Alex had told her where to find me. She glanced around nervously, and in a whisper, asked if she could talk to me. I joined her in the hall, and tried to read her eyes, but was unaccustomed to making sense of what was going on inside the mind of an attractive girl. To make matters worse, she wasn't saying anything. We stood together, shy and awkward, with nothing more to talk about than if we were complete strangers.

She left, and in order to figure out what had happened, I asked Alex about her. He was pretty sure Sheri was in high school, or maybe a dropout. Our liaison drifted into the past, a milestone in my life that looked a million times more impressive in the future than it did now.

Losing my virginity turned out to be no different from having it. Girls seemed just as unattainable, and I felt just as anxious about them as ever. It was all incredibly confusing. My longing seemed more frustrating than ever. *If sex wasn't the solution to my loneliness, what was?*

§§§

I sat in the library, trying to force knowledge into my mind, but my concentration drifted. The library seemed so dull, with students silently reading. When I walked across to the hustle and bustle of the *Rathskellar*, the huge cafe at the Student Union, everything opened up, with crowds, noise, music, and above all, anger against the war.

I supposed the students with short hair were talking about shallow things like friendships or their schoolwork. I was only interested in students with long hair and blue jeans, whose bitter diatribes filled the air. We were going to change the world, and we were going to start by changing ourselves.

Music played an increasingly important role in my anger against the system. When I went to the record store, I entered another world, a world in which lyrics would answer all my questions and music would arouse new, exciting emotions that would help me cope. I bought albums by the Beatles, the Doors, the Rolling Stones, the Mamas & the Papas, and Ritchie Havens, and listened to them over and over in my room. Music lifted me into a different part of myself, and each new album seemed to generate even more psychic power than the one before.

My mind rang with refrains from Jefferson Airplane's song *White Rabbit*. "One pill makes you larger, and one pill makes you small." Their hints at the mind-altering effects of hallucinogenic drugs felt like a call from another dimension, and even though I had never taken LSD, I felt an urgent need to explore alternate forms of consciousness. When I attended live jazz concerts or played jazz albums in my room, they took me on a trip even more intense than rock and roll. Without lyrics, their angry music made me feel that I had left the world of adult responsibility far behind. Music united me with my peers. We were crying at the world to leave us alone and let us do whatever we wanted.

I continued my lonely journey through math and science classes. My grades kept dropping but I no longer cared. I had a hard time remembering what inspired me during the first year. Instead, I poured myself into the second semester of my art history class, trying to understand the images people had created throughout history.

Art history class had progressed from ancient art to the churches of the Middle Ages. I had never been inside a church. They always seemed foreign and dangerous. However, the ones in my art history books felt uplifting and beautiful. Their high, vaulted ceilings, flying buttresses, fantastic gargoyles, and statues of saints made me forget the politics, power, and cruelty that often accompanied religion. These buildings enraptured me with glorious human creativity and longing.

As hard as I tried to learn about the way the world works through art and literature, many areas of life still seemed out of reach. I couldn't understand girls. And, just as important, I couldn't understand the dangerous power wielded by the government. I agreed with the left-wing students who said the ruling classes had always been greedy and controlling. I knew with increasing certainty that society was messed up and I wanted to tear down everything that the government and the corporations stood for. Our constant refrain of "Stop the war" made me feel part of an important movement, but knowing what I hated had not helped me understand where I was going.

Like a Rolling Stone

As the end of my second year approached, I tried to figure out what I should do for the summer. Returning to a research job in Philadelphia felt like I would be going backward. I needed to learn so much about the world. Simply stuffing my mind with more medical facts seemed like a waste of time.

One day, Alex told me he was going to take a charter flight to Europe. As soon as I heard the word *Europe,* my mind sprang to attention. During this last year, my study of European art and culture led to deeper understanding on so many levels. I had seen posters advertising charter flights, but until this moment, it didn't occur to me that I could actually take one.

"So what's the deal?" I asked.

"The plane drops you off in Belgium, and then ten weeks later, you get back on the plane and come home. For everything else, you're on your own."

His plan seemed intriguing, and yet incredibly vague. "What are you going to do when you get there?"

"I don't know," he said.

"But where are you going to start? You must have some idea."

"Definitely Paris."

My mind raced. Paris! French art was so interesting. And I had studied French in high school. I was fascinated by France. I wanted to do this.

"And I might go with Cary to Turkey," he continued.

"Turkey scares me," I said, imagining an untamed country with a lot of drugs and people who didn't like Americans. I didn't add that Alex's friend Cary also scared me. He took harder drugs and said more destructive things about society than I was comfortable with. I wanted to keep my distance.

"Why don't you come?" Alex said. "We can stick together as long as it works and split up if we want."

I bought a book called *Europe On $5 a Day* and learned about international youth hostels and how to buy cheap meals. I called my parents and told them I was going and that it would be really cheap. They were not wealthy, but were committed to supporting me through college, and apparently their commitment included a summer in Europe.

While I was making plans, I bumped into Devin, the guy I ate dinners with earlier in the year. He mentioned that his friend Carl would still be in Italy after his semester abroad. I wrote to Carl and we agreed to meet on Elba, a vacation island off the coast of Italy. Now I had my plan for the summer. Hang out with Alex as long as possible, visit Paris, see lots of museums and churches, and visit Carl in Elba.

The charter flight that summer of 1967 was filled with students from Wisconsin, a few of whom I recognized from the Student Union. We landed in Belgium and I picked up my backpack from baggage claim, excited by the adventure ahead.

Hoisting my pack onto my back, I said to Alex, "So where are you heading, man?"

"Cary and I are going to Holland," he said. I realized they had already made plans, and if I wanted company I would have to tag along.

"OK. Great. I'll come with you."

He shrugged. "Sure, man. If that's what you want."

Finding our way to the train station, I wondered about these people, speaking other languages. They all seemed so interesting. I wanted to meet everyone and see everything. On the train ride to Amsterdam, I watched the countryside roll by.

Amsterdam was old and quaint, and the slightly guttural quality of Dutch voices seemed so exotic. The row homes were hundreds of years old, and their quaint architecture and the many canals made the city seem so exotic. I walked around, soaking in as much as I could.

The pastel-colored money even made small purchases of snacks seem curious and fresh. We visited the art museum, rich with paintings. I couldn't believe my eyes—here were some of the originals that I had seen in my art history book. I stared at each one, trying to see beyond the surface into the heart of the painter. I felt that my presence here in front of each painting was momentous, a historical connection between the painter a hundred or more years ago, and me.

By the second day, Alex was spending more time with Cary. On the third day, he said, "We're leaving now."

As he walked away, I realized I was alone. I felt only slightly betrayed. In high school I entertained myself by walking around historic Philadelphia, looking at the buildings and people, and when I was tired, I read. I could do the same thing here.

One difference was that in Philadelphia, I never considered going into a church. In Europe, they became my sanctuaries. Each time I walked into one and looked up at the high vaulted ceilings and breathtaking stained glass, I felt like I had traveled to a more peaceful place. I sat and soaked in their beauty.

After a week in Amsterdam, I took the train to Paris and rented a room with dingy wallpaper and a sagging bed. Then I went out to explore. I walked past houses hundreds of years old, visited museums, feeling lifted by their beautiful paintings. Even though I had been inside dozens of churches, I felt inspired each time I entered a new one. I visited famous Parisian sites such as Montmartre, the Bastille, and the river Seine. These experiences brought to life sights and sounds that had lived in my imagination for years.

Whenever I needed a break, I pulled out a book and read. I did this in restaurants and on park benches. At the end of each day, I returned to the seedy hotel room and in the glare of the bare bulb, I lay for hours. I had a list of books that I wanted to read, important books that would help me understand European culture.

Journey to the End of the Night by Ferdinand Celine appealed to my belief in the darkness of the twentieth-century. His fragmented, depressing sentiments made me almost sick with despair. I leaned into Celine's perspective hoping that his brilliant expression of the human condition would help me understand my own pessimism.

I also read novels by Samuel Beckett, author of the absurdist play *Waiting for Godot*. His novels were rich in language, and terrifying in their depiction of decrepit bodies and meaningless lives. Each page armed my intellect with the message that nothing we do has any value. Reading his books took me deeper into myself, which was perfect for a summer when I was ending up almost entirely alone.

One evening, feeling cooped up, I went out to walk around. The streets were bustling with night people and I passed a man with an attractive woman on each arm. He caught my eye and stopped, swinging around so both of the women were facing me. In French he asked me if I wanted one. I thought I must have misunderstood him. I had no idea why a man would walk around offering his extra girlfriend to a stranger. Now all three of them were looking at me, waiting for my answer. I looked at the girls. They were really pretty. Too nervous to make sense of what was happening I felt like they were fictional characters who had been dropped into the wrong story. I laughed nervously, and said "Non, merci." The man looked at me and shrugged, and they turned and continued on their way.

How strange it all seemed. Just a few decades earlier, authors and painters from all over Europe congregated in Paris looking for inspiration, among them my hero, Samuel Beckett. Then German tanks rolled in, and the Gestapo ruled these very streets. Now, I was standing in the middle of what looked like a street-party. As the guy with the two girls receded into the crowd, I couldn't understand what I had just done. After being invited to the party, the only thing I could say was, "No, thank you."

I quickened my pace and returned to the hotel, walked through the courtyard, climbed the stairs to the dingy room, turned on the single lightbulb, lay on the sagging mattress, and picked up my Samuel Beckett novel. Here I was in his adopted city of Paris, and I had just received a lesson reinforcing his point that life is absurd.

After two weeks in Paris, I took the train to London. On the train, an American told me about a flat where some British students were allowing students to sleep in their living room. I knocked on the door and was greeted by a woman, perhaps a couple of years older than me, who said I was welcome to sleep on the floor. There were a few of us crashing, but the people who ran the place were clean cut, going off to classes every day, and living a normal life. I was so withdrawn I only used the place to flop, rather than make friends. I went out every day and repeated the routine I had started in Paris. I must not have been much fun to live with, because when the students kicked me out of their apartment, they were courteous but firm: "This is more than a request."

It was too soon to meet Carl, my friend from Wisconsin, so I headed to Florence, Italy to take in the museums and churches. As I walked around the streets of Florence, I turned down a side street and stepped into a café, hoping for a drink of water. When my eyes adjusted to the dim light, I saw a row of wizened old men sitting on barstools, in front of them, tiny demitasse cups. Whereas the museums and churches recorded the past on canvas and in stone, these men, barely moving, looked as if they had been sitting here for centuries, preserving the past in flesh and blood.

By now, my lonely, nomadic lifestyle was wearing me down. Spells of diarrhea and a relentless sense of hunger made it increasingly difficult to enjoy the cultural treasures. The entire summer had been a search for peace, but wherever I arrived, I looked around and discovered that peace was somewhere else.

Soon it was time to pack up and move on to my next destination, the Island of Elba. Its sunny Mediterranean beach was filled with Italian families but no one spoke English, not even the shopkeepers. And Carl wasn't due to show up until the following day. With no museums to visit, I felt lost. The first evening, I walked around carrying my pack and then slept on the beach. I didn't take many showers that summer, but it didn't matter. Since the first week in Holland with Alex, I was on my own.

When Carl showed up at our appointed time, I felt so relieved. He pulled out some dope and we got stoned, staring out at the ocean, talking about Madison and life. The sun was so hot and the beach, so beautiful. With the help of friendly conversation I finally felt at peace. When our visit ended, I took the train back to Brussels, where I would meet Alex and catch the charter flight home.

I should have been upset with Alex for leaving me alone, but after we said hello, he offered me some of his hashish. I decided I was happy to have him as a friend, even though he was not always as predictable as I wished. But what good would hash be now? I didn't want to get caught with it crossing through customs. Rather than throw it away, I swallowed the dark, sticky blob.

When the plane boarded, I ended up sitting next to one of the cutest girls at the university. I heard she worked part-time as a fashion model. I was flattered that she was willing to sit next to me, but her beauty completely jangled my nerves. After we took off, I looked at her and started hallucinating. In my vision the whole world exploded into beautiful bright pools, like a brilliant emanation that started through her but then built into crescendos that left me breathlessly in love. My behavior must have given me away. Despite her initial pleasant smile when we first sat down, for the rest of the trip she avoided my gaze and refused to speak to me.

As we approached New York, the plane tilted down and I became convinced we were crashing. I had to restrain myself from screaming. At first I thought everyone else would start screaming, too. Then, despite the alarms inside my mind, I focused on the stewardess. Watching her carefully, I couldn't detect any trace of concern. Finally, I convinced myself that if she wasn't afraid, I shouldn't be, either.

When I went through customs, the clerk asked me to take everything out of my pack and place it on the table. I pulled out the scruffy underwear and shirts that had been on me all summer. His mouth drawn tight, the agent wouldn't touch my stuff. I saw myself through his eyes and I remembered that people who belong to "the system" hate us as much as we hate them. With a look of disgust, he waved me on and I was back in the States.

Before heading back to Madison, I stopped in Philadelphia to visit my parents. I knew it would be difficult. During the summer, without even realizing it, I had become increasingly enraged against those who went to work every day and supported the war.

My old bedroom felt strange, like it belonged to a younger, more confined boy than I had become. *I don't belong here anymore.* To pass the time, I bought a couple of records and listened to them over and over. Bob Dylan's lyrics supported my anger. He said that if you weren't busy being born, you were busy dying. The phrase screamed in my mind. No one around here seemed to be busy being born, and I was feeling more and more disconnected.

That Sunday, we went to visit my aunt and uncle in the Northeast section of Philadelphia, just as we had done many times when I was growing up. I walked up the stairs to their home, just as my Uncle Ben was coming down. When he saw me, a look of horror crossed his face. I always loved Uncle Ben's cheerful manner, but I was a little suspicious of him, too. As the owner of a clothing factory, he had a lot more money than the rest of us, and sometimes came across as aloof. Now, when he saw me, with my long hair and bushy sideburns, he quickly looked away and without meeting my eyes said in a loud voice, "I didn't know we had anything like that in the family."

I was shocked. *How could he say that? Was he so caught up in capitalism that he would reject his own flesh and blood?* I wondered the same thing he had voiced: *I didn't know we had anything like that in the family.* I couldn't believe my cheerful uncle identified so thoroughly with this corrupt war-making society that he couldn't see through its façade. Now it was my turn to look at him with disgust. I didn't say it out loud, but I thought, *Screw you. I don't need you. This whole system stinks.*

The one person who might understand was my boss at the medical center, Dr. Rusy. His easygoing nature and his kindness to me when I worked there made our relationship seem warm and special. Before I headed back to Wisconsin, I stopped in to say hello. The medical center, just a few blocks from Dad's drugstore, felt like home. But when I poked my head into Dr. Rusy's office, instead of a congenial smile, his face turned into a mask of horror. Finally he said, "What have they done to you?"

I stammered a hello. He recovered his poise, and asked me how I was doing, but I was already hurt. I told him I was OK. The meeting was short, and when I walked out to the busy street, I had to admit that even Dr. Rusy didn't understand. *What is wrong with these people?*

My Third Surge into the Crowd

I returned to Madison in the fall of 1967 for my junior year, feeling just as unnerved by the mob of 30,000 kids as I had the two previous years. This fall, though, I had an additional challenge. I didn't even have a place to sleep.

I must have been crazy to leave campus at the end of last semester without lining up a place to live, but with my roommate Mark transferring to a school in his beloved New York City, and my other roommate moving in with a different group of friends, I was on my own. Now, I was going to have to scramble.

After a swim at the Armory to soothe my nerves, I headed back into the crowd that always swarmed through the halls of the Student Union. When I spotted someone I knew, I asked if I could crash at their pad. I hated begging for a place to stay but I had no choice. A few people greeted me, and apologized that they didn't have room. Finally, a girl I met the year before came over to me and said she heard I was looking for a place. I could stay on her couch.

It was a second-floor apartment directly above a popular ice cream shop on State Street. I looked around at the furniture in total surprise. It was clean and colorful with a comfortable-looking sofa, unlike any apartment I had seen in Madison. Nothing looked dark, broken, or dirty. Did students really live in normal looking apartments? The thought had never occurred to me.

As soon as I deposited my stuff in her living room, I felt edgy, penned in. I told her I had to go. She looked shocked. "You just got here."

"Sorry. I have to find a place," I said, heading for the door.

My real reason for leaving was that despite the crazy energy of the crowd, I felt more comfortable around a thousand people than I did alone with a girl.

I returned to the Student Union, bought a cup of coffee, and sat in the *Rathskellar*. Thousands of students streamed by on their way to and from classes, stopping to drink coffee and chat. As usual though, as soon as I started talking to one, I began scanning the room to see whom else I could find, and soon excused myself to walk around again, as if the person in front of me was never enough. Each one seemed too individual, too small. I wanted to connect with all of them at once — at least the ones with long hair.

When I finished my coffee, I forced myself to push away from the gravitational attraction of the crowd into the relative quiet of the hallway, where I scanned a bulletin board plastered with war protest announcements, flyers for poetry clubs, and roommate-wanted ads. I answered one of those ads, for a place close to campus.

Don, the boy who would be my apartment-mate, had short hair, and his pants even had a crease. I was barely able to hide my contempt. But the room was spacious, with a large window that looked out upon the high-rise dorms where I stayed when I was a freshman. When I met the other roommate, my resistance faded. Jason had a bushy beard and long hair. I signed the contract and moved in.

One of the most important items I retrieved from storage was my record player. I lovingly placed it on a shelf, strung wires to the speakers, and dropped the needle onto the new album by the Doors. One song frantically urged us to set the night on fire. Yes. That was exactly what I wanted to do. But how? I played the album over and over, trying to let myself go into its wild passion, hoping I would "break on through to the other side."

On campus, we gathered by the hundreds to hear talks about the pointlessness of the war, and how it benefitted the corporations who made weapons. By revealing the flaws of society we would discover the truth. Alex was often at the rallies, too.

Like me, he seethed with anger against the system. Perhaps he could help me understand what to do with all these feelings. Once when we were talking about the protests, he said, "You know the locals hate these protests. They think they're run by Jews."

His idea troubled me. Why should they care if some of us were Jewish? We wanted to promote peace and justice, not religion. If a lot of us happened to be Jews, that was just a coincidence.

Or was it? The more I thought about this connection between Judaism and the war protests, the more sense it made. Maybe Jews were willing to stand up to governments because we had been persecuted by so many of them.

The sensation I felt at war rallies reminded me of the horror I felt when I read about the Holocaust. How could civilized governments have convinced their citizens that it was OK to set aside the most basic of all decencies, the rule not to murder your neighbors? Governments violence against their own population had always provoked in me a sense of revulsion that started at the base of my spine and made me want to scream.

I wondered if the reason I felt this anger so deep in my body was because I had inherited it from my grandparents. They had fled the soldiers who raped and murdered Jews in their Russian villages. Even though they never talked about it, I imagined it had been transmitted to me on some invisible wavelength. We were linked across generations by the age-old question, "Why couldn't good people rise up and stop the bad?" That's what we were going to do. We saw the murder, and we were going to stop it now.

To understand how societies work, I became obsessed with one of the books assigned in my class on social psychology. The book, *One Dimensional Man* by Herbert Marcuse, claimed that modern corporations could make more money if consumers all thought the same way. To shape our collective thinking, corporations devised a devious partnership with the media. With the help of newspapers, radio, and television, corporations had turned us into shallow, one-dimensional people.

Through Marcuse's eyes, I could see that corporations weren't just convincing us to buy specific products. Their goals were much more sinister: They were shaping our approach to life.

I read and reread Marcuse's brilliant analysis, underlining key points and pondering the truth of his words. Reading the book made me feel I was in the presence of a genius who was revealing the mysterious inner workings of society. It also made me feel more depressed.

His ideas pounded like a jackhammer, chipping away my faith not just in the government, but in the whole system. I came to understand that all institutions were designed to manipulate my sense of self. I wasn't as independent of a thinker as I had believed. *If they controlled my mind, who was I, anyway?*

My agitation after reading Marcuse's *One Dimensional Man* was similar to the way I felt after reading Sigmund Freud's *Civilization and its Discontents*. According to Freud, individuals are in a constant tug of war between the rule of authority and their ever-present sexual pressures. From Freud's point of view, life is hell and it's going to stay that way.

Marcuse based his sinister view of society on a different struggle — that between individual creativity and corporate power. His conclusion was that corporations were winning. And like Freud, he didn't offer a solution. Marcuse, too, seemed to be saying life is hell and it's going to stay that way.

If these great thinkers couldn't offer a method to stop the downward slide of civilization, how could I? The only hope lay in the anti-war rallies. With all of us working together in the protest movement, we could call attention to the problem and begin finding a solution.

When the speakers at rallies ranted against the atrocities of war, we blamed the corporations who profited from that war. And to protect their right to continue making money, they were destroying our souls. When we threatened to block buildings, we were obeying a sense of obligation not only to protect society, but also to protect our individuality. We couldn't turn back history to stop Hitler's mass murders, but at least we could stop the injustices in our own time.

Shattered

On my way to class in late October, someone handed me a flier, which showed a photo of an infant disfigured by burns after Americans dropped jellied gasoline on a Vietnamese village. Representatives of the company that manufactured the ghoulish weapon were on campus recruiting employees and we were going to protest.

I detoured over to the heart of the campus to see what was going on. A crowd had already formed on the grass in front of the Commerce Building and a speaker was shouting that it was time to take a stand. We were going to enter the building and stop them from conducting job interviews. This seemed like a good way to make a statement so I headed inside where hundreds of us packed the hallways. A protest leader with a bullhorn said, "Lock your arms together. Don't let anyone through." I knew the girl next to me, not by name, but I had seen her around campus. We exchanged a few comments, at first excited by our mission.

But the scene outside grew increasingly ominous.

Through the plate glass window I saw scores of policemen. They wore thick padded vests, helmets and facemasks, and they carried three-foot long clubs that made them look even more frightening. I had never seen this level of police activity around a protest before and wondered if they really intended to break in here. For the first time since the protests started, I considered the possibility that I might get in trouble with the law. I heard of kids in other colleges being dragged out of buildings but I never thought it would happen here.

The armed men moved closer, gathering just outside the doorway. They had snapped their masks over their faces. I was only a few dozen feet from the front and couldn't believe what was happening. Were they really going to use force? Surely they'd compromise. My companions grew quiet.

Shouts came from outside, and after a pause, the man with the bullhorn said, "The police have agreed to back off for five minutes." His voice sounded strained, as if he didn't believe what was happening either.

I turned to the girl next to me. "Is that the best concession they could get? I thought these negotiations would drag on for hours. Five minutes?"

But we didn't have to wait that long. Within seconds, the room exploded with the sound of shattering windows, followed by fellow protestors shouting in anger and fear. Cops poured in through the jagged opening, stepping over shards of glass and swinging their clubs. Just a few yards in front of me, students were falling, or trying to break ranks and get away from the onslaught. I only had a few seconds to react. I turned to look for an escape route, but the crowd behind me blocked my way. When I turned back I was looking into the eyes of a cop, his club raised ready to strike me. Time stopped, and in that split second, he shifted his focus and struck the girl next to me. I recoiled and joined the mad dash to the exit at the far end of the hall.

Outside, we gathered in the courtyard, facing the police who had amassed in front of the doorway. The crowd grew as more students stopped to see what was going on. Ambulances lined up to take injured students to the hospital, and now, instead of protesting a distant war, we were furious about armed men clubbing unarmed students right before our eyes.

Chants arose from the chaos. "Pigs!" we screamed in unison. Then someone shouted, "Cover your face." Caustic gas burned my eyes and nose. *Another outrage!* We ran away gasping. When the gas dissipated, we surged back to the front of the building. The crowd continued to swell as word spread across campus. Then another chant erupted. As if possessed, we shrieked in unison, *"Sieg Heil, Sieg Heil,"* our arms snapping straight with each repetition mimicking the goose-stepping soldiers of Hitler's Third Reich.

Thousands of us screamed *"Sieg Heil"* at the tops of our lungs. It felt so terrifying and violent. I had seen newsreels showing tens of thousands of German citizens screaming the awful benediction to their commander-in-chief. They used their slogan to affirm their intention to destroy all that was good and holy about life: "We will follow you into the darkness. We will murder innocence."

Our shout today was not an affirmation but a curse. *Curse you, all of you who would destroy innocence. Curse you who would wage war. Curse you. Curse you. Curse you. No more. No more.*

Our good intentions couldn't go back in time to stop or undo what Hitler's minions had done. But perhaps if we screamed loud enough and hated viciously enough, we could stop these armed soldiers standing right in front of us.

The crowd continued to grow, pressing me from behind, when a surge pushed me so hard I was forced forward into the police line. The cop a few feet in front of me lost his balance and started going down. Other uniformed men rushed to his aid. It all played out in slow motion, as I struggled to maintain my own balance. Somehow the cops regained control, and something in me began to crumble.

What's the point? They don't care. This protest changes nothing. Their guns and corporations speak louder than our idealistic dreams. I felt utterly drained by fear and anger, my mind numb with emotions about police and war and violence.

I drifted away and wandered off campus, aimlessly at first, looking around at the streets, whose dark autumn gray reflected my despair. I headed toward Alex's apartment hoping that being around him would help me make sense of what was going on. But I was disappointed to see his scary friend Cary there.

When Cary saw me come in, he said, "When the cop went down, I had my hand on his gun. I could feel the trigger." His bragging about touching the gun disgusted me. *What was he thinking? He could have destroyed everything. We're not murderers.* I mumbled an excuse and left.

Alone at my place, I dropped a record on the turntable, lit a joint, and sat in the dim glow of a candle. My whole world had crashed in just one day. This morning, I was filled with hope that our idealism would win. Tonight, I feared the protests were sucking me into the war machine, invading my psyche, creating violence within me just as intense as the violence I was trying to stop. I didn't want to attack people and I didn't want to be attacked. I hated the war just as vehemently as ever, but I had lost my interest in acting out against it.

The next morning, I replayed the memory of the policeman with his club raised over my head, the horror and betrayal I felt, and our pathetic attempt to fix it by screaming. The cycle awakened my own terror of history, an emotional loop of fear and humiliation: blacks and slavery; Jews and the Holocaust; and now war protestors and cops. The war machine had grown more dangerous. In addition to wanting to send me into the jungle with a gun, now they were sending police to beat me and threaten arrest.

The police needed to clear a path for the recruiters so they could staff the war machine. I could see more clearly than ever that Herbert Marcuse was right: We were being manipulated by corporations.

I couldn't bring myself to attend my physics and math classes, adding the sickening throb of guilt to my already overwhelmed emotions. The one class I continued to attend was Social Psychology, because the professor was young and hip and let us talk about the chaos out on campus.

I stood up during one class. "It's just like Hitler," I sputtered, and sat down feeling foolish and humiliated. I hated speaking in public but I had to say that.

The rallies continued, but the drone of their message no longer made me feel powerful. Instead, the rebellious words felt like a mockery. We could protest. Hand out fliers. Try to block buildings. Nothing would change. The police would always win.

Finally, when anyone tried to offer me a flier, I put my hand up and kept walking. I didn't need to see that picture of the burned baby. It had entered my soul, mixed with cops and clubs, riots and tear gas. My inner turmoil drowned out the outer noise. I felt the underpinnings of my sanity stretched to the breaking point.

Fraying Connections with My Past

As I boarded the plane to Philadelphia, I tried to brush aside images of mobs screaming at police and fleeing teargas canisters. Flying home for Thanksgiving felt like going backward through a time machine, from crowds of protestors to the quiet Jewish neighborhood where everyone thought the world was exactly the way it was supposed to be.

When Mom greeted me I couldn't look her in the eye. When Dad came home from the drugstore late at night, I struggled to say hello. I went to bed wondering if I should have come home at all.

The next morning, Dad tried to make conversation. "How's school going?" His question triggered a cascade of angry thoughts.

"Do you have any idea what's going on?" I screamed. "How could you ask about school when our government is burning babies at this very moment? The school is just a pawn in their game."

I was so disgusted and angry I didn't even look at him, sitting there in his middle-class home. He didn't say anything, but my thoughts kept exploding. Finally, I blurted, "The world is going to fucking hell, and you're part of the problem. That drugstore is part of the capitalist system, and you're a capitalist."

I couldn't believe the words that had just thundered out of my mouth. I knew the drugstore supported the family and was sending me through college. Serving customers had been one of my main reasons for wanting to be a doctor. But the world no longer seemed so simple.

I ran to my room and stared at the six-foot-wide black-and-white poster of Pablo Picasso's painting, *Guernica*. Its disjointed images of warriors and women, babies and spears were a perfect protest against the horror of war, a horror that I had been feeling deep in my gut ever since high school when I first saw pictures of dead Jews piled like trash in a liberated concentration camp.

My grandparents, in their Russian village, had suffered, too. Then their luck changed when they came to America. But now, my own country was creating more suffering. Did living here mean I was participating in bombing women and children? Was I now one of the perpetrators? I had to break free from this never-ending cycle. But how?

At least in Madison, I was part of a movement, united by our hatred for war. In this house no one seemed aware of the pain that Americans were creating in a foreign land. Here I felt like a fragment, a broken chip of glass with sharp edges—fitting into nothing.

§§§

Mom yelled up the stairs. "Jerry, Grandmom and Grandpop are here."

I shuffled into the swirl of greetings. Grandpop, with his soft eyes and dark olive skin, looked at my outsized bushy hair and wide sideburns that covered the sides of my face. "I like your hair," he said with a twinkle in his eye. Grandpop always had a big smile for us kids. I couldn't be angry with him. He had moved to the United States to escape persecution. He was one of the oppressed people. He wasn't my enemy.

Grandmom greeted me with a pained look. But that wasn't surprising. She almost always looked tense. While Grandpop headed to the sofa with a drink in his hand, barely taking the trouble to hold up his head, Grandmom was in constant motion. And when she did sit, her posture was ramrod straight.

I loved her diction, which sounded more polished and crisp than anyone I knew. I thought she would make a good radio announcer. In her youth she had taught immigrant Jews how to speak like Americans. She didn't succeed with her own husband, who still routinely switched his w's and v's. I doubted either of them cared about the Vietnam War or even knew much about it. Instead of making me angry, this thought made me wonder what it would feel like not to worry so much.

When we sat at the dining room table, its holiday china piled with food, I was still upset about my one-sided confrontation with Dad. I muddled through the turkey, stuffing, potatoes, and pumpkin pie, but couldn't taste any of it. Nor could I enter into the family conversation. Dad didn't have much to say, either. I couldn't wait for everyone to leave so I could get back to my room.

After dinner, Grandmom said she just happened to have her music with her. Her comment signaled our family ritual. She always happened to have her music with her. "Oh really?" my mother said. "Since you have your music, perhaps you would play us something."

Grandmom responded coyly, "Are you sure?"

Everyone except me laughed. She sat at the piano, with her regal posture, leaning forward to flip through the dog-eared

75

sheets of music, many of them repaired with pieces of tape. I had heard this collection of Broadway tunes and classical pieces for as long as I could remember. She selected one, and began to play the lively music. As her fingers moved across the keyboard, the tension drained away from her body. She almost looked like a little girl.

After she finished, she paged through the pile again, as if searching for just the right one. Then she played my favorite piece. The Yiddish title *Bei Mir Bistu Shein* meant To Me You Are Beautiful. The fact that the title was in Yiddish made me smile every time I heard it. Even though my parents only spoke Yiddish when they wanted to keep secrets from us kids, I loved listening to the sound of their words. Occasionally, Yiddish cropped up in unexpected moments of intimacy. When I was little, Grandmom or Grandpop would lean down, pinch my cheek, and say, "What a *shayna punim* you have," a phrase that meant something similar to this song's title. "You are so beautiful." The expression made me feel warm and safe.

Pouring herself into the upbeat tune, Grandmom's body bounced lightly, her shoulders bobbed, and her hands danced across the keys. Burning babies and riot police may have been screaming in my mind, but they weren't screaming in hers.

Grandmom's music and body language seemed to be saying, "Don't worry about it. We're okay." Riding on her joy, I accepted the possibility that the world wasn't completely falling apart.

When the song ended, she stood and turned to face us. With a comical smile and a sparkle in her eye, she took a formal bow. Everyone laughed, and I laughed too. Soon, I'd be back in my hell of worry and anger. But for this moment, I could just be with my family, even my capitalist dad.

Groping Toward Survival

With the demolition of my belief that we were going to stop the war, I became unclear about why I was alive. I was even beginning to lose faith that physics would teach me the laws of the universe. The elegant power I found so appealing in my high school and freshman physics courses had been based on simplistic assumptions. But the advanced courses included real-world considerations such as friction. With these factors added in, the simple, sweet calculus equations broke apart into a cumbersome series of corrections and approximations.

In one lecture the professor explained how the tides rise and fall depending on the motion of the moon. After entirely filling a blackboard with equations, he raised it on tracks and continued writing on the blank board behind it. By the end of the lecture, his writing completely filled six boards. Those mysterious tides that awakened wonder in poets throughout history sank beneath the weight of convoluted equations.

"Give me Truth, not this mess," I thought magnificently, as I put my head down on the desk and passed out. When the bell rang, I stood up and filed out with the rest of the students. No one looked at me with surprise. I had done the same thing many times before. Because of my solid background in calculus, I passed the course in Mechanics, but I was worried about all these other types of mathematics that were being introduced.

§§§

During the spring semester, I joined a food cooperative, the Green Lantern, located in a shabby converted storefront. Hip people, almost all males, ate dinner at a reduced price in exchange for helping prepare food and cleanup afterward. Other than eating dinner surrounded by familiar faces, my social life continued to consist mainly of short conversations with passing acquaintances.

One bright spot was the friendship I developed with my bearded roommate, Jason. When I was with him, I didn't need to be so intense about everything. Like me, he enjoyed trying to make sense of things, but his method seemed less complex than mine. Perhaps the fact that he grew up on a farm in Wisconsin gave him a simpler approach, as if by reading the crops, and the rainstorms, and life close to nature, he could see into the causes of things more easily than I could when seeing life through books. I became increasingly comfortable with him, as if we had known each other forever.

I gravitated to another gentle Midwesterner, Roberta. Tall and attractive with a deep throaty voice, she bypassed my confusion with women by clearly signaling she had no interest in romance. We spoke as friends rather than potential lovers, a unique approach that put me at ease. Even though we only saw each other when we happened to cross paths on campus, her friendship offered a welcome break from my otherwise lonely existence.

To help me survive my increasingly difficult physics classes, I signed up for a math class called Fourier Analysis. Up until then, I had been accustomed to visualizing each individual mathematical equation, as if it were one whole puzzle. Solving the puzzle gave me a surge of satisfaction. The branch of mathematics called Fourier Analysis presented an infinite series of equations, each one of which was an infinite series. Like walking into a crowded room and not being able to decide which person to relate to, so I couldn't relate to any of them, this new math presented a crowd of problems, each one begging for attention, so I couldn't figure out how to solve any.

Feeling overwhelmed by these crowds of equations, I barely studied, I missed classes, and I didn't bother doing the homework. I had always managed to pull it off before. The night before the final exam, I sat in the library forcing myself to stay awake, but all I could do was stare helplessly at the textbook. Taking the exam felt like a nightmare, attempting to see series of equations through a fog of fatigue. For the first time, I failed a course. I was devastated. If I flunked too many courses, I wouldn't be able to stay in school.

At the end of my third year, Roberta said she was moving away after she graduated. Even though we were only acquaintances, I hated losing her stalwart presence. It didn't seem fair that she was leaving.

I felt an even greater sense of loss when Jason told me he was moving to Berkeley, California. Our friendship had given me a sense of peace I had not felt since I had arrived in Madison. I asked him why he was leaving. "I love California. The girls are pretty and it's always sunny."

These two people had given me glimpses of hope in an otherwise gloomy year. Now they would both be gone. I wondered why I was staying here. But someday I might be thankful for this college degree. And anyway, where would I go? I felt so disconnected from my family and past, I no longer knew where to find my home.

A Disturbing Summer

I decided to stay in Madison during the summer of 1968 and take a course called Mathematical Computing, a topic that combined my love for mathematics with the power of computing machines. To qualify for the course, I needed to have already completed a year of Computer Science courses. I ignored the requirement, figuring I learned enough about programming from the non-credit class I took at the University of Pennsylvania in high school.

I was correct about one thing. I loved the way they explained how to solve mathematical equations with computers. But when I attempted to write a computer program, I couldn't figure out how to operate the punch card machines, or what codes I would need in order to submit my job to their mainframe. Even the simplest assignment felt like I was running through a maze, hitting walls, backtracking, and then running in a different direction. As usual, I only wanted to do a minimum of work, so I quickly fell behind.

Once again, the campus in summer felt like an abandoned movie set, with trickles of students attending classes in almost-empty buildings. So I was surprised one day to pass a group of students sitting on the grass, talking in loud voices. It didn't look exactly like a protest rally, but they were excited about something. I asked someone at the edge of the gathering what was going on.

"Carloads of boys are coming to campus and beating up students with long hair." I was accustomed to hearing people gather to rant about the war, but this was different. In addition to anger, I now heard the raspy tones of fear. "They think we're all New York Jews," she continued.

There it was—Jews again. Why would anyone care enough about my religion to want to beat me up? I suspected she was being paranoid. This was the United States. My grandparents had come here precisely because it was the one country on earth where we could be accepted. And why was I even saying "we"? I wasn't from New York and barely considered myself Jewish anymore.

Another one in the group said, "They're trying to stop our protests. We have to stick together."

This was another reason why their concerns had nothing to do with me. After the riot last year, I no longer took part in protests. I decided to ignore the whole mess.

I arrived home, planning to smoke dope and listen to music. At the doorway of the apartment building, I encountered my downstairs neighbor, Elias. He greeted me in his thick Greek accent. Perhaps he noticed the loneliness in my eyes. As I turned to go, he said, "Joan and I are going to walk into town tonight for some ice cream. Do you want to join us?"

I hesitated. I typically stayed away from guys with short hair, but Elias was different. He studied physics at Harvard, which meant he was brilliant beyond measure. I loved his deep Greek accent, which made me wonder about growing up in a foreign country. And during the past year, he had been kind to me, explaining a math concept with which I was struggling. His girlfriend, Joan, was stunning, which was another incentive to accept his offer. Finally, I decided that socializing with normal-looking people wouldn't be so bad. "Sure," I said. "That sounds like fun."

We headed into a sweltering night, almost as hot as the day. On the busy street near the state capitol building, I heard someone shouting. I assumed it was just some random noise but Elias said through clenched teeth, "Just keep walking. Don't turn around."

I didn't understand why he sounded alarmed, so I looked back and saw five boys. One of them was closing in on me. A bulky guy with short blond hair, who looked to be sixteen or seventeen, faced me with his hands up as if he were boxing. *What is he doing?* Without thinking, I started yelling at him to get away from me. He lunged forward, grabbed me around the waist and threw me down.

I felt myself fall, with him on top of me. I was so surprised I didn't have time to register pain. As if in a dream, I watched the others swarm in and kick me in the body and head. From my vantage point on the ground, I saw Elias ask them to stop. A boy punched him in the mouth. Joan started screaming. Passing cars slowed down and honked, and then one of them pulled over. It was the getaway car. The boys jumped in and drove off.

Elias helped me stand up. His lip was bleeding. I felt horrible that he should be hurt trying to protect me. He didn't even have long hair. In a few minutes the university police came and took our statements. Joan gave them the license plate number. How cool-headed. She had written it on her hand. Then the cops drove us to the university hospital.

I complained to the intern that my head hurt. He laughed. "Of course it hurts. You were kicked in the head." His lack of concern angered me. Perhaps for him it looked no worse than a barroom brawl. For me it was a horrible violation. I insisted on an X-ray and just as he predicted, nothing was broken. Another problem was my missing contact lens. Without it, I could barely see.

Elias and Joan left hours earlier, so the two policemen drove me back to the scene. After the protest last fall, I thought of police as enemies. Now, they shined their flashlights at the pavement and helped me look. Even though we didn't find the lens, I felt an unexpected flush of gratitude toward them. By the time I arrived back at my apartment, dawn had begun its march across the morning sky.

Over the next few days my headaches lessened and I replaced my contact lens. But the emotional wound wouldn't heal. When I was out at night, every time a car approached, I slunk into the shadows, ducking into doorways or behind poles, hoping no one could see me, hoping I could still my racing heart, hoping they wouldn't throw me down and kick me.

I armed myself by carrying a motorcycle chain in a book bag. I practiced slamming the heavy chain against the fence outside my apartment, crushing someone's imaginary skull, getting them off of me, pushing them away. But I also felt foolish, knowing that without ever having been in a fight, I would have no idea how to actually use the thing.

A longhaired student who I recognized from protest rallies approached me in the Student Union and said he heard what had happened. I nodded, too disgusted with the event to say much about it. I wanted to forget the whole thing. The student kept talking. "There's a lawyer on campus, Mel. He's one of us. You ought to go see him."

"I can't afford a lawyer. What could he do, anyway?"

"Ask him yourself. He's sitting right over there." He pointed to a guy with long red hair and a beard. He looked like a nice enough guy. I went over and told him about my situation.

"That's a bummer, man. We can sue the bastards. Stop by my office and we can get started."

When I went to his office the next day, he explained that they had inflicted damages on me and that I could sue them in civil court to pay for my expenses and suffering.

"You don't have to pay me. My fee will come from splitting the settlement."

"OK," I said. Suddenly I liked the legal system. With a lawyer by my side the law would work on my behalf.

Since Joan had written the license number of the getaway car, Mel easily tracked it down. My attacker was the son of a small-town police chief. I imagined the family sitting at dinner, with Dad ranting about New York Jews destroying the country, and after hearing this hatred long enough the son decided to do something about it. I wondered if the boy's actions horrified the police chief or made him proud. I was more confused than ever. The purpose of the protests was to save boys like this from getting killed in a senseless war. Now they left the safety of their homes to come and hurt me.

The police chief didn't make much money. The most Mel could settle for was $75, which we split 50-50. It felt good to receive even this symbolic amount.

§§§

I stumbled through my computing course, skipping classes and smoking too much dope. I slipped by with a C. Elias accepted a teaching position in Washington, D.C. and moved away at the end of the summer, another potential friend lost.

I dreaded the surge of returning students in September and wondered if I could keep going. I was heading into the home stretch of my college experience, feeling like I had the wind knocked out of me — deflated and scared.

Falling Deeper into Depression

When the masses of students returned for the fall semester, the attacks stopped, but I continued to imagine phantom assailants in every passing car. In addition to these fears of physical assault, I was also concerned about my schoolwork.

With only two more semesters to go, I had to fulfill all the requirements for my major. I knew there were some difficult courses ahead, but I still relished the possibility that I would learn something new. One topic that intrigued me was Einstein's theory of relativity. So far I had only studied the simpler version, called special relativity, which showed that when velocity approached the speed of light, space and time were distorted. There was another, harder version of Einstein's theory called general relativity. This version showed how gravity exerted by a large body distorted the fabric of space and time.

I was in awe of Einstein's ability to mathematically describe such complex mysteries and I wanted to see what he saw. But so far, every time I tried to understand this advanced theory, the knowledge slipped away. This was my last chance but no specialized course on that topic was offered this year.

I thought perhaps a hip young physics professor, Robert March, might be able to help. I went to look for him at the dreary bar where he regularly hung out. He was sitting alone, and when I introduced myself as a physics major, he barely looked up, lost in his own thoughts. The smell of alcohol and the flickering red and blue neon beer signs made me feel queasy, but I kept talking.

I told him I was hoping he could be my advisor in an independent course.

"What do you want to write about?" he asked, looking at me more closely.

"I want to understand the difference between special and general relativity."

"That's a hard paper," he said, his face brightening.

"I'm fascinated by Einstein's deconstruction of time and space. I'll do a good job."

He told me he would be happy to sign the necessary papers. I was elated. Perhaps learning something new would rekindle my interest in school.

I took a book out of the library, planning to dive into the independent study course about relativity. From the introduction I learned that Einstein's almost visionary understanding of physics had enabled him to precisely predict the way huge gravitational pulls would actually change the shape of space. However, inside the book each page was filled with symbols that made no sense. Now I understood why no one had explained this topic clearly. To do so would require new, specialized mathematics. What had I gotten myself into?

§§§

Most evenings, I stayed in my room with the lights low, smoking dope and listening to music. Now that I was smoking regularly, I easily slipped into the flow of the music, sometimes seeing the notes like swirls of color, fitting together in patterns. Each instrument stood out, distinct from the others, so when I listened to a band, I could follow the violins with one part of my mind and the trumpets with another.

When I played a symphony by Beethoven, I felt lifted by the vast sweeps of sound, reaching toward heaven. Other times Leonard Cohen's dismal, poetic plaints moved me almost to tears. I agreed with Bob Dylan's raves against the status quo, his voice wavering on the border between anger and tears. And the sad, desperate pleas for love of blues singers like Billie Holiday made me realize I was not the only person who felt such deep sorrow.

Many of my albums were rock and roll with catchy guitar lines and exciting beats. Sometimes I sat still and listened, losing myself in the music as if I was on a ride through my mind. Other times I stood up and moved, using my body as if it were an instrument. I experimented with parts of my body—for example moving my knees in time with the drums and letting my hands lift and sway with the movement of the violins, or I would hold my knees absolutely still while dancing wildly with every other part of my body, or just dance with my shoulders without moving anything else.

When I heard about a party, I went alone, hoping to find a girl whose intensity about dancing matched my own. When I found a single girl gyrating to the music, I asked for a dance. Most of the time, the girl declined, or danced one song then excused herself. I always went home alone, confused and depressed. I didn't understand what I was doing wrong.

During the past year, Alex had broken up with his first girlfriend and was now together with Kristen. She too had pale skin and light brown hair. But unlike Alex's first girlfriend, who was often sullen and distant, Kristen had a smile that started with her lips, spread to her face and eyes, and then radiated throughout the room. We laughed a lot together and when she asked me how I was doing, her rich alto voice made me feel like I was part of the family. Sometimes I hung out with them at their apartment. Other times we went together to the *Rathskellar's* cabaret to listen to their musician friends perform jazz.

Alex's musician friends were often kind to me, thanks to the many hours I had spent with them at the record store and at their performances. But his actor friends responded to me with distant eyes and unsmiling faces. When Alex and Kristen were sitting with their actor friends, I didn't stay long.

One night, I was at Alex's apartment. "Hey, man. Kristen and I are going to get stoned. Do you want to join us?" Usually getting stoned meant smoking marijuana. This time he was holding out a pill.

"What is it?" I asked.

"I don't know. A friend gave them to me. They're supposed to be good."

I had never taken pills, afraid of the effect they might have on me. I heard too many horror stories about bad trips and feared that if I had a bad trip, the lingering effect could last for months, or worse, could fry my brain altogether. Kristen smiled her big, warm smile at me, and in that moment, taking a pill sounded like fun. I swallowed it and soon felt my perception shifting into a blurry, pleasantly confusing swirl. I felt even closer to them, and more protected than ever, as if I were bathing in an ocean of love.

"Come on," Alex said. "Let's go for a walk."

We walked to the Student Union and weaved our way into corridors behind the theater. Finally we entered a room that I didn't even know existed. Their actor friends, including many I had never seen before, were gathered in a circle. They all turned to greet Alex and Kristen, but they turned away from me. Then, one of them shouted at me, "Hey, what are you doing here? You don't belong here." Others joined in. I was still basking in the cloud of love I'd felt just before we entered and at first I enjoyed the attention. This was the most interaction I ever had with any of them. I guessed they were doing some sort of acting exercise. If I could figure out how it worked, maybe I could participate.

I looked at each one and said, "I'm here to be with you. I'm here as one of you." But they were too quick for me. As soon as I tried to speak to them, they changed the game and shrank away, ignoring me, pretending I wasn't there. That's when the pain began.

In the altered state induced by whatever drug I had taken, I felt an overwhelming sense of rejection. I told Alex I needed to leave, hoping he and Kristen would come with me. I was disappointed when he said, "Go ahead, man. We're going to stay here."

The air rushed out of the bubble of love that had surrounded me just a few minutes earlier, letting in all the loneliness I had ever experienced. I walked around campus in the most despairing night of my life. I ended up back at my apartment, screaming at myself in the mirror, and trying to smash it. Finally, in desperation, I searched through my drawers for one of the Thorazine pills I had stolen from my father's drugstore. I heard it was supposed to get people down from bad trips. I swallowed it, praying for relief. Within a half hour, darkness seeped into me, making me feel as if I was alive in body, but my spirit was completely dead. Eventually I fell asleep.

When I awoke, I struggled to make sense of my bad trip. What had begun as a great adventure in consciousness and love turned into its opposite. Whether the pill was acid or something else didn't matter. The bad trip had a lasting effect, just as I had always feared. That horrible rejection and betrayal lingered in my mind, a fitting entry into the dark, cold season of my last winter in Madison.

§§§

Like every other winter I had experienced in Madison, the temperature plummeted by the end of November and kept going down. Temperatures below zero degrees Fahrenheit froze the moisture in my nose the moment I walked outside, into the perpetually gloomy light of the gray sky. Through the winter, I fell into deep isolation, skipping classes for weeks at a time. I smoked dope, listened to music with my eyes closed, or danced in front of the mirror. Brilliant novels like Charles Dickens's *Bleak House* reinforced my dark mood.

My despair was fueled by a powerful connection with jazz. I sat alone, stoned, feeling my way deep into the dark corridors of Monk and Coltrane, not even bothering to look for a way out. Their choppy saxophones and clarinets created fragments of melodies and then smashed them into pieces inside my mind, and their bass lines felt like a roadmap to hell. I wondered if their music could destroy me.

An acquaintance at the *Rathskellar* saw me looking gloomy. "Hey, man," he said, "None of this really matters." I looked at him wondering why he was smiling while telling me this depressing news. He said he was trying to cheer me up. "It's all an illusion, man."

I had heard this perspective before. People often returned from acid trips claiming that everything is an illusion. Since high school I knew that modern physics made essentially the same claim, mathematically proving that physical reality wasn't as real as most of us supposed. I always viewed these paradoxes of modern physics as weirdly fascinating. It never occurred to me they were particularly uplifting.

In my desperate state of mind, I wondered if these ideas could help me feel better. To learn more, I picked up one of the books by Alan Watts, an author whose ideas about Buddhism had been popular on campus. Reading the book, however, didn't answer my questions. I couldn't reconcile the notion that life is an illusion since it all felt so real.

I returned to my physics books, hoping to make more sense of Einstein's mathematical description of the fabric of space and time. But the books left me no wiser about this esoteric subject than when I started. I simply lacked the background to understand these equations. I would have to take an incomplete grade in my independent study course and come back to it later.

Light at the End of the Tunnel?

I sat alone among the crowds in the *Rathskellar*, researching a paper about Marshall McLuhan. He had become something of a celebrity on campus, and I was trying to understand his futuristic claims. According to him, television was turning the whole world into one community.

The concept of a global village reminded me of my grandparents trying to blend into the American Melting Pot, as if they could turn the entire country into their new village. They had fled Russian, but they weren't really Russian. That country just happened to be the latest stop on their centuries-long odyssey, hounded from one place to another by neighbors who didn't think they fit in. McLuhan's notion of a global village provided me with a new perspective on their forced march. I felt a glimmer of pride that my ancestors sampled cultures all across Europe. They had been citizens of the global village long before the United States even existed.

McLuhan, though, did not base his theories on the movements of people in mass migrations. He was more interested in mass media, which connected us with each other from the comfort of our living rooms.

During my years in college, I had become increasingly convinced that the world was falling apart. Marshall McLuhan offered the stunning possibility that everything was falling together. His futuristic ideas seemed so crazy, leaping from one thing to another. I wasn't sure if he was a charlatan or a genius. But I had to admit, the ideas appealed to me.

Whenever I pulled out my schoolwork, I guiltily brushed past the book about statistical thermodynamics. In simple thermodynamics, we calculated the transfer of energy from one body to another. But statistical thermodynamics attempted to describe the way trillions of molecules transferred heat. To track this level of detail, I would need to learn yet another type of mathematics. Until I did so, I would just barely be able to solve the problems associated with this course. Hopefully I would understand by the end of the semester.

In the midst of these bleak times, I occasionally struck up a conversation with Devin, the guy I knew from sophomore year, who had once shaved off half his beard. He, too, was in his senior year, and by now he had found some interesting alternatives to campus life.

Some guys he knew lived on a farm. One of them was the boyfriend of his ex-girlfriend or something like that. The thing these guys had in common was their interest in motors. They all tinkered with cars and motorcycles. Ordinarily, I would have had no interest in guys who loved motors, but Devin's enthusiasm was contagious. As the harsh winter started to break, he invited me to visit the farm. I jumped at the opportunity to get out of my horrible rut. On the drive, I asked Devin why these guys lived in the country. It seemed so far away from all the action on campus. He said, "It's cheap and wide open. You'll see."

When we arrived, I saw a barn surrounded by dozens of cars in various states of repair. Someone was riding a motorcycle around a rutted dirt track. Inside the barn, a guy was standing in a mechanic's pit, peering up at the underbelly of a car.

Devin introduced me to Frank, who had a trimmed red beard. After we moved on, Devin said, "Frank is really smart. He's a graduate student in computer science. A lot of these guys are engineers and scientists." I saw the place in a new light, as a sort of intellectual playground for smart people.

On our way back to campus, I could feel the walls of student life closing in on me. For almost four years, I lived in the midst of thousands of students, without ever figuring out how to relate to them. Now that I'd seen what it was like living outside town, I was intrigued. My tiny apartment felt like a prison. I wanted to get out.

Devin's passion for vehicles suddenly made sense. He took me to find a car, and for $75, I drove away in a Chevrolet station wagon. Then I looked at the campus bulletin boards for off-campus apartments and found a room in a farmhouse about fifteen minutes outside of town. The guy who had placed the ad had shorter hair than the people I typically wanted to be around, but he would just be a roommate. I had no intention of socializing with him. He didn't mind my long hair so I moved in. Instead of being surrounded by crowded apartments, I was living among recently planted fields.

Devin also convinced me to buy a used motorcycle, saying that with spring approaching, we could ride through country roads together. He suggested a Honda 305 Superhawk. The motorcycle was sleek and the polished chrome engine casing made it feel like a shiny toy. I wrote a check, knowing my dad would replenish the account.

When I first attempted to start the bike, I struggled to hold it upright. But once I was underway, I turned the throttle and felt the bike surge forward. When Devin and I roared past the farms and big sky of the Wisconsin countryside, I screamed in delight with the wind pressing my leather jacket against me.

As the weather warmed, I went for a walk across the rich, plowed farmland behind the house, accompanied by my roommate's shorthaired dog, Luke. That sunny day, surrounded by fallow fields, everything seemed possible. The tension of my mind released into the gentle breeze. When we passed a stand of trees, Luke spotted something and bolted. I shouted and ran after him. He had cornered a tiny baby fox, huddled in a crouch, shivering with fear and courageously hissing at the barking dog towering above him. I pulled Luke away and as he went bounding off to the next adventure, I felt shaken by the close call.

I looked around, with nothing but countryside and farms as far as I could see, and felt scared for the little fox. This was his home, but it was filled with danger. I began to feel scared for myself, too. There was a much bigger world than the college campus and I had no idea how I would fit in.

As the end of my senior year approached, I peered into the future and saw only vague possibilities. I knew I didn't want to stay in Madison. The winters were brutally cold and I didn't like the fact that people kept leaving. Maybe I would go to Boston. It was on the east coast, which felt familiar. But I didn't know a single person there, and since it was hundreds of miles north of Philadelphia, it would probably be cold.

Or maybe California. Jason had written a couple of times and told me how much he enjoyed the balmy sunshine and people of Berkeley. And California was the place where hippies were finding a new way to live.

I would figure that out by the end of the summer. I couldn't go anywhere yet. The disjointed paragraphs of my paper looked just like McLuhan's books, with fragmented ideas strewn haphazardly across pages. But I doubted my professor would appreciate the irony. Instead of turning in my incoherent essay, I took an incomplete grade, intending to finish it during the coming summer.

I still needed to finish the research paper about the general theory of relativity. That was a second incomplete grade. And the course in statistical thermodynamics turned out to be every bit as hard as I feared it would be. There was no way I would pass the final. As the semester came to an end, with finals just days away, I filed for an incomplete for that, too.

I rode my motorcycle out of town to the farmhouse in shock, trying to imagine yet another summer in Madison. The campus would be empty of course, as it had been every summer. And I would be on my own, finishing schoolwork and trying to figure out my future.

Then Alex phoned me. He was heading to California, because a friend of his had asked him to drive a car there. "Why don't you come with me? I could use the company."

"Sorry Alex. I can't leave now. I still have a final next week. You go ahead without me." Despite almost four years of wanting to be around him as much as possible, I felt relieved that I wouldn't be able to go. I was afraid if I left, I might lose the momentum I needed to finish my incomplete grades.

Alex replied, "I'll wait."

I hesitated, wishing he had said he was going without me.

"Well, if I did come with you, I really can't stay long. Are you sure you're coming right back?"

"I'm absolutely sure. It's only a week. Come on, man."

Giving in to the pressure, I said OK. I justified it by thinking I needed a break and it could be a good adventure.

Continuing the Revolution in California

Berkeley, 1969

After 24 hours of driving, we were only halfway across the vast expanses of the American West and I wondered if the 2,000-mile drive to San Francisco would ever end. To ease the tedium, we smoked some hash, but that only amplified my claustrophobia. By the second day, my mind was screaming. I just wanted to get out of the car.

Too broke to stay in a motel, we turned off the highway and parked on an isolated side road. I climbed alone onto a wooded hill and lay down on a bed of pine needles. Around me I heard whispers of wind and creaking trees. My mind raced faster and faster, imagining snakes, bears, and creatures without names. Huddled in the dark, I fought for hours with a free-running bout of panic. When the sun came up, I returned to the car and told Alex what happened.

He laughed. "Yes, I hate wide open spaces too."

His comment eased my paranoia and reminded me that despite our differences, our shared East Coast heritage made it easy for us to understand each other.

Nearing our destination, we crossed through the barren Nevada desert, when out in the distance rose the skyline of Las Vegas, a shimmering mass of metal and glass. We stopped for lunch, and walked through a casino, chilly as a refrigerator, noisy with the whacking and ringing of slots. Everyone seemed to be in an altered state, enraptured by dice, cards, or the wheel. These people seemed to be worshipping money, hypnotized by the possibility of putting out their hands and scooping up more. I was more eager than ever to visit California, where the hippies were blazing a new trail, where money would no longer play an important role.

As we approached California our fear of the police escalated due to the rumor that California hired the meanest, angriest cops in the nation. We took care to obey the speed limit, but before long, a police car pulled up behind us with his flashers on. "Oh, God," I screamed. "He's going to kill us." When we pulled over I jumped out of the car on the passenger side, and surreptitiously threw my tiny stash of hash into the ditch, praying he didn't see. Then joined Alex on the driver's side.

The cop looked at us and said in a tone of surprise, "Do you boys know you're dressed in the same clothes as prisoners?"

"No, sir," I said, fascinated as much by this observation as by the almost kind tone in his voice.

"Yep. Blue jeans and blue cotton shirts."

He peered into the car, and then went back to his patrol car to check our plates while I tried to decide if I liked looking like a convict. That didn't seem to be exactly the image I was aiming for. It turned out he had no real reason to stop us, and let us go without a ticket.

When we reached our destination, an apartment in San Francisco, Alex's friends from Madison greeted us in loose fitting, brightly-colored clothes. They offered us lunch, and we sat on the floor at a round table made of rough-cut lumber. The meal consisted of a small serving of rice and salad, barely enough to relieve my hunger. Trying to make conversation I asked about the odd-looking table.

"It's an empty cable spool we liberated from a construction site," our host said. "Living in California, we've learned to take advantage of the abundance all around us."

After lunch we went for a walk around San Francisco. Just as I imagined, we were surrounded by young people, dressed in hippie clothes, with long flowing hair. My culture shock was complete when I saw a few girls wearing gauzy, see-through blouses. In addition to the heart-thumping reminder me that I still didn't have a girlfriend, they also completed the impression that I had landed on another planet. So far, I had seen differences in diet, clothing, and furniture. It felt as though California was inventing its own culture.

The next morning, eager to visit my old friend Jason, I took my backpack and hitchhiked across the San Francisco Bay to Berkeley. The town reminded me of Madison, teeming with students. But in addition, there was the addition of hippie guys wearing beards, and girls with long hair and flowing clothes. I kept walking until I found the tidy row home where Jason lived. A beautiful dark-haired girl opened the door and offered me my first radiant California smile. I melted inside, and stammered. "I'm a friend of Jason's. Is he here?" She invited me in and went to find him. I noticed a couple of people asleep on the living room floor.

Jason came up from the basement and hugged me. Boys in Madison never hugged each other, so here was another new bit of California culture.

"I was meditating," he said, eyes twinkling.

"That's nice," I answered, without knowing what meditating was. He was always experimenting with ideas, so I smiled, ignoring his comment, just glad to see his friendly face.

"Did you meet Susan?" he asked, gesturing to the woman who answered the door.

"Briefly," I said, turning to take another drink of her dazzling smile. Jason laughed. "She and her husband own a health food stand on campus, so we always have lots of fresh sprouts and yogurt." I was beginning to think everyone in California was a vegetarian.

He offered me lunch, which consisted of brown rice and vegetables and lots of sprouts. I asked why their diets were so different from what I had always eaten.

"We're very conscious of what we put in our bodies," Jason said. "Meat is bad for physical and spiritual health ... all that killing," he said, looking disgusted.

I was intrigued. Californians even had a philosophy about eating. Other than the kosher dietary laws in my childhood, this was the first time I heard of anyone thinking about what foods they put in their body.

The kitchen opened onto a small porch, where I saw a skinny guy sitting cross-legged, stark naked, except for the long straggly beard that hung down his chest. His eyes were closed, and a beatific smile played across his lips.

"Who's that?" I whispered.

"Oh, that's Paul. He worships the sun."

"That's nice," I said. Jason said he meditated, and now this. I wondered if I would ever understand some of the zanier aspects of this place.

"Come on. Let's go for a walk," Jason said. "I'll show you where John sells his natural food."

We walked up the hill chatting about how life had been since we'd last seen each other the year before. He was working at a produce market, and I told him that I was uncertain about what to do after college. The bright sun, balmy breeze, and friendly conversation slowed time. Instead of incessantly worrying about where I needed to be, and what I needed to be doing, being here in this minute felt perfect.

Jason said, "It looks peaceful now, but this is the street where they had the big People's Park protest last year."

"I don't know anything about that. I've been so preoccupied in Madison."

"Students staged a huge march in order to convince the university to allow them to grow a community garden. The administration called in the National Guard. For months there were armed soldiers all over town."

"Oh my God!" I exclaimed.

"It escalated and one day the soldiers fired live ammunition into the crowd. One guy was blinded by buckshot."

I felt a wave of nausea, remembering the day when the police turned against us in Madison. I tried to imagine these streets filled with protestors. All they wanted was a garden. Soldiers? ... Shots fired into the crowd? ... What horrid betrayal they must have felt.

Trying to push the image out of my mind, I looked around at the peaceful setting. None of that violence was evident here at the majestic gate that marked the threshold between Telegraph Avenue and the campus of the University of California. The hubbub of students made me feel like I was in Madison, surrounded by the wonderful energy of young people trying to learn, but here the weather was much nicer.

Jason pointed to a small, cheerfully painted cart with a sign that said, "Fresh Squoze Juice." A guy with a neatly trimmed black beard was busy serving lunch to a line of college kids. When there was a break in the line, Jason introduced us and John flashed me a warm smile.

"What can I get you?"

"I've never had carrot juice," I answered.

"You'll love it," he said, handing me a cup of the frothy orange liquid. As I took the first sip, the sweet aroma of carrots penetrated me to the core.

Sitting out in the sun for a while, amid crowds of students, I felt a sense of friendship and peace. Berkeley was lovely. I asked Jason if there was any room for me to stay at the house for a week until I could get a ride back to Wisconsin. He said, "I'll ask John. I don't think he'll mind you crashing at the house."

The next afternoon John and Susan walked into the kitchen, dressed up as if they were going out.

"We're going to a party. Do you want to come?"

"Sure," I said. I was always up for a party. I enjoyed dancing and even though I was convinced I would never find a girlfriend, I thought I might as well keep trying.

The house was up in the hills above Berkeley. With a commanding view of the San Francisco Bay, and high above the fog that so famously rolled in below, these houses were larger and more beautifully landscaped than the ones down by the campus. John said, "Have you heard of the book, *I'm OK. You're OK*? The author of that book owns this house."

The place was packed with well-dressed people, making me self-conscious about the holes in my frayed blue jeans. I couldn't think of anything to talk about, so I followed the loud music that rose from the basement. Down there, everyone was dancing so I did what I always did at a party. I looked for the most energetic dancer and asked if I could cut in.

In this crowd, the best dancer was easy to spot. She was taller than almost any girl I had known, almost as tall as my own height of six-foot-one. She had straight blond hair down to her shoulders, a round face, and she was really moving. I walked over and leaned in, shouting above the din and popped the question. "Sure," she smiled, and we started up.

Fueled by the energy she was returning, I became entranced in the motion and danced faster and faster. A guitar player in Madison once told me, "Your head is moving in sixteenths." While I had no idea if it was true, his tone of admiration made an impression on me. I knew I was moving at least that fast tonight.

With her sophisticated moves and obvious pleasure in the dance, she kept up with me, and then she said, "Wow," and in a theatrical gesture, sat down on the floor, in the midst of the crowd, to gawk. This was bad because it meant she wasn't dancing, but good because she was staring at me with a warm glow on her face.

I pulled her up and we danced more. At the end of the song, I shouted, "I'm Jerry."

"I'm Patricia," she shouted back. After a half hour, a girl with dark hair came up to Patricia and said something I couldn't hear. Patricia turned to me and introduced her sister, Carol, who gave me a warm, friendly smile. The guy who Patricia had been dancing with earlier was also standing there. "This is Peter. He's just a friend." Peter's smile was not nearly as warm as Carol's.

After an awkward pause, Carol said, "Come on, we have to go."

As they were leaving, I said, "Where do you live?" Patricia told me the name of the street but not the address. "It's only one block long," she said, and they were gone.

First Love

Back at Jason's that night, I slept on the floor of his room in the basement. When I woke the next morning, all I could think about was Patricia. Her innocent smile, her blondness, and her spectacular dancing had grabbed me and wouldn't let go.

I hitchhiked over to the other side of Berkeley, and when I found the street, my heart danced. I walked up and down under shade trees, every breeze showering speckles of bright sunlight across the sidewalk. When a woman emerged from one of the houses, I asked her if she knew a tall blond girl named Patricia. She pointed to a door. I knocked and the woman who answered said, "She lives downstairs."

The apartment she directed me to had its own entrance off a small veranda on the side of the house. I was nervous now, and walked up to the glass doors, not sure what I would say but wanting to see her face again. No one answered. I knocked again, but still nothing. I just stood there in this quiet space—a warm sun, and wind rustling through the leaves above. It was a perfect moment. I found a scrap of paper and wrote a poem.

"Seeing far,

being even farther from your heart,

my own.

Light in dark.

Wrest the spark,

from so still a day."

I stuffed the paper in her door and left. The next day, I returned, my heart pounding hard. She was there and greeted me with that wonderful smile.

"Hi," I said. "We met the other night."

"Of course. It's so nice to see you." She stood at the door smiling, but looking uncertain. I couldn't believe I was being this forward.

"I was here yesterday. Did you get my note?"

She looked confused.

"I left a poem on a slip of paper."

"Oh, that's what that was," she paused. "Do you want to come in?"

The small studio apartment included her bed and a crib for her toddler son. She saw me looking at it. "Brian is with his grandmother today."

She was lovely to look at, the tall blond I had dreamt of my whole life without realizing it. I stayed for tea, and we talked. She said she was just getting ready to go swimming and asked if I wanted to join her. We drove up into the mountains above Berkeley. I turned around to see the gorgeous sunshine across the San Francisco Bay. We got out of the car at a quiet lake. We were almost the only ones there. We swam around and when I bumped against her, her touch shot through me like lightning. In that moment, I realized she might want me, too.

That night after Brian went to sleep, we slept together. This was it! This was where I wanted to be. For the first time, I loved someone who returned my affection. I never wanted to leave.

Her sweet smile and cheerful voice lifted me out of my depressing thoughts about the world, which was strange considering that her life had been torn apart by tragedy. She had married her high school sweetheart, and gotten pregnant just before he shipped out to Vietnam. As a conscientious objector, he didn't carry a gun and was only in 'Nam for a few weeks before a bullet ripped through the Red Cross insignia that medics wore on their helmets. He never met his son.

Recently she had hooked up with a lawyer who was away for the summer on some sort of internship. She said she wasn't in love with him. I told her I loved her. The next night, we made love again. She looked at me, the electricity so strong between us I thought it could light the heavens. Finally, she said I could stay. I was so excited. A girlfriend at last.

All my stuff was in the farmhouse in Wisconsin. It was safe for now. And my incomplete grades could wait. I called Alex, told him to go back without me, and moved in with Patricia.

We lived for several months in bliss. I wanted to be near her, touch her, and watch her every moment. I stopped obsessing on my anger against the system and instead obsessed on her. I frequently stared at her and listed all the things I loved. Her body, of course. It was long, and golden, and feminine. Once she sketched a silly cartoon of her home and us in it. The drawing awed me, as if she possessed some artistic life force I would only ever know by loving her. She could dance. And she was a mom who knew how to take care of a baby.

Once she came back from a visit with her Catholic mother who told her Jewish guys really take care of their women. Even though I wasn't sure what this meant, I was flattered. It was the first time I had heard of a non-Jew saying good things about us.

I flew back to Madison to collect my stuff and ship it out to California. Then I went back to be with her. She had some money from her husband's veteran benefits and we decided to move into a larger apartment. However, despite what her mom said about Jews, I had no idea who I was or how to offer myself as a real person. I had just come from sixteen years as a fulltime student. I had never worked a job and didn't even know why I should ever work. I was stumbling along each day with no direction, and my love for Patricia didn't change that.

At first, she didn't mind that I had no idea what to do with my life or how to help her take care of her baby. Then one day, I reached out and touched Patricia's skin, warm and inviting. As I leaned over to kiss her, she stiffened.

"What's wrong?" I asked.

"What are we doing?" There was a hardness in her voice that I had never heard before.

"What does it look like we're doing? We're in love. Isn't that enough?"

"I'm thinking about my son," she said, tears welling up in her eyes.

I knew I was no father. But it was worse than that. I couldn't even relate to adults unless they talked about intense concepts like Reality or Meaning. What was I supposed to do with this little boy?

"What *about* him?" I said, feeling a wave of defeat. She had never raised him as a topic of conversation like this. "What are you saying?"

"He needs some stability. I want to provide him a home."

"What do you want me to do?" I asked.

"I don't know. Don't you think you need to get a job?"

"Is that what this is about?" I asked, shrill and angry. "How could you bring this up now? Everything is going so well."

Jerry Waxler

The Berkeley sunshine drained out of the room. We didn't even have our clothes on yet. Just moments earlier, I thought everything was perfect. Now, her simple question awakened a cauldron of angry thoughts. I couldn't understand how I could feel so close to her and so confused at the same time.

"I've been trying to sort myself out," I said. "I don't know what to do."

The old darkness started closing in on me. From a dreamy morning with the woman I loved, I was sliding back toward the confusion I felt when I left Madison. I had come here to join the hippie rebellion, to live free and find a way out of the mess adults had gotten us into, and now I was supposed to get a job? It made no sense.

"I think I'd better go," I said, pulling on my blue jeans.

Patricia looked at me. "Where are you going?"

Without saying goodbye, I finished dressing and walked out into the Berkeley sunshine.

The rhythm of walking among the students and hippies usually lifted my mood, but today my misery built on itself, making my sorrow heavier with every step. All my years of thinking that life is absurd and unjust came crashing back. I realized that reality is too dark to sustain such bliss for long.

After hours of walking, I ended up at Jason's house, where I first arrived in Berkeley, less than a year ago. I knocked.

John opened the door. "Hi Jerry."

"Is Jason here?"

"He moved back to Wisconsin."

I swallowed hard. I stood there on the doorstep, glancing up and down the perpetually sunny street. I was hoping Jason's soothing presence might give me strength. Now he was gone, too. I was on my own.

"Do you mind if I crash in his room until I find a place?" I asked.

"Sure," he said. "That would be fine."

Feeling as though I was carrying out my own execution, I went to tell Patricia I was moving out.

Last Try

Even though I no longer had any reason to stay in Berkeley, I had no reason to be anywhere else, either. The only option that made sense was to find a place to live. I answered an ad for a cheap room only a few blocks away from campus.

A young couple in a one-bedroom bungalow showed me the room, in what at first appeared to be an old shed behind the house. On closer inspection, I saw I would be living in a garage that had been partitioned down the center by a wall constructed of discarded doors. One half of the garage was being used to store furniture and boxes. The other half would be my room. Through the gaps at the bottom of the wall, bamboo grew into my room, providing character to the otherwise dingy space. The only furnishings were a mattress, a small table, and a lamp. I would use the bathroom in the house. I said I'd take it.

Growing increasingly depressed, I sat alone and listened to melancholy music. My favorite was *Needle of Death* by Bert Jansch, about the hell of heroin addiction. His despair went so deep it felt like a hunger for death that called to me and drained away all hope.

To express the enormous surges of my own emotions, I wrote poetry. Each word felt precious and powerful, but I didn't know what to do with my writing. Could I publish it? I had no idea. Through the school newspaper I found a poetry group and attended a session. A dozen clean-cut students sat around a table and a teacher led the meeting.

When it was my turn, I read my poem aloud. One of the students quoted a passage and asked, "Why did you use that particular word?"

"Because that's just the word that came out," I snapped. "That word belongs there."

The room grew quiet.

"Our rule is that no one can use that excuse," the teacher said. "If you want to discuss your poetry with us, you need to tell us what the words mean and why they are there."

I didn't know what to say. What right did they have to question one of my words? Who did these people think they were? They continued to talk about my poem, but I stopped listening. *Coming here was a mistake.* I left as soon as I could and never went back. From then on, I only wrote in my room, alone, and kept the poetry to myself.

I became more withdrawn than ever, going for days speaking only to the cashiers at the supermarket or health food store. Most of the time, I sat alone and read. On the rare occasions when I smoked dope, instead of feeling high, I felt more confused, and if possible, even sadder. Finally, I realized that marijuana was only making me feel worse, and I stopped.

After a few months, an element of realism crept into my thinking. I probably couldn't live this way forever. Someday I would need to make a living. And if I had to make a living, perhaps I could return to the only job that made sense—to become a doctor. I wondered how I could revive that old dream. Even though my grades had collapsed, I hoped that with diligent work I could restore my academic record. I just needed to take a few more pre-med courses and to pull up my grades.

I lived a ten-minute walk away from one of the premiere public universities in the country. By now I was a resident of California, which guaranteed cheap tuition and easily available student loans. If I could get into UC Berkeley, I would be back on the road toward my true destiny. This glimmer of hope about becoming a doctor excited me, as if I were returning home after a long exile.

My heart quickened as I set to work. I walked to campus and picked up the application. I hoped that my high aptitude tests and my early academic potential might convince the admissions board that I had been waylaid and was ready to get back on track. Because of my passion for math and science, the engineering school would be the most likely place to grant me admission. I wrote an impassioned essay about how I wanted to be a doctor to help people and do my part to improve the world.

I had not yet earned my bachelor's degree, but I discovered that might actually be an advantage. Because I didn't yet have a degree, I was entitled to enter as a full-time undergraduate student, which would make it easier to receive financial aid.

The more effort I made on my application, the more confident I became. I knew this was going to work out. It had to. And it did. The engineering college accepted me. I would soon be back on track to apply to medical school. My future was again clear. I would use the summer sessions to help ease me back into the routine.

In the first summer session, I enrolled in Comparative Embryology. I looked around at the other eager pre-med students who were taking the class. After four years competing with the incredibly smart boys in Central High, I wasn't worried about staying on top. I remembered the powerful feeling of going to the library at Temple Medical School and studying textbooks as if they were novels and looked forward to lighting those intellectual fires. I just needed to get out of my slump.

To keep my energy high, I resumed my habit of regular, intense exercise. In Madison, with its brutally cold winters, swimming in the indoor pool was ideal. In Berkeley's eternally pleasant weather, running was more convenient. Every day, I jogged around the perimeter of the field where the football team trained. Their presence made me feel less alone, and inspired me to run harder.

To enhance the experience, I took off my shoes and ran barefoot. With the grass ticking my toes, and the air caressing the rest of me, I felt like I was flying. After the run was over, the pleasure lingered for an hour or two. When I came down from that high, I started thinking about Patricia and feeling overwhelmed by life. I could barely wait until the next day's run when I would be to let all of this go.

The Comparative Embryology course taught me the detailed steps through which the single cell of an egg develops into a fully formed body. Two cells, four cells, eight cells, at first, all are identical. Then they rapidly begin to differentiate into specialized cells that would become organs and limbs. I remembered a phrase from high school that echoed in my mind like a mantra: "Ontogeny recapitulates phylogeny" meaning that each human embryo repeats the entire cycle of evolution, from tadpole, to fish, to mammal. I loved the rhythm of those three words, like poetry. My awakened curiosity gave me hope. If I could tap into the drive I felt in high school, I would be unstoppable.

The word "comparative" in the course's title meant that I would need to learn about the development of a whole range of animals. However, I diligently kept up with my schoolwork and got an A. The achievement filled me with pride. I was on my way.

In the second summer session, I took Comparative Anatomy. The anatomy course offered no insights into bodily processes. Instead, I had to cram my brain with an endless stream of information about skulls, spines, ribs, and toes, of fish, birds, reptiles, and mammals. The tedious attempt to memorize body parts filled me with fatigue.

My lack of enthusiasm showed in my final grade of B. The failure to achieve another A crushed me. *I have to focus*, I told myself. *Everything depends on it.* No longer in school, my only way to distract myself from depressing thoughts was with exercise. I woke up the next day and prepared to go for a jog.

But instead of the thrill of anticipation through mind and body, as I was accustomed to feeling before a jog, my limbs felt like dead weights. I dragged myself toward the field, trying to understand this unfamiliar feeling. When I walked onto the grass, I managed a half-hearted half-lap, and then, just sat down. I couldn't find the energy to continue. I turned around and walked home and slept all day. The next day was worse. Fatigue permeated every fiber of my being. For the first time in my life, I didn't even want to walk around campus, let alone run. If I couldn't maintain my energy, I would certainly fail.

I went to the student clinic, assuming they would identify the problem and cure it. But blood tests revealed nothing, and since they couldn't find anything wrong, they couldn't help me. I couldn't believe my bad fortune. My plan to restore my academic momentum had encountered an unexpected and terrifying obstacle.

My entire life hinged on this one issue and I didn't know where to turn. Desperate for relief, I thought about Peter, the man who accompanied Patricia to the party the night I first met her. He was a therapist who did a type of deep muscle massage called Rolfing. Supposedly it released negative energy stored in the body. Since Patricia and Peter were friends, I hoped that visiting him might also have a healing influence on my troubled heart.

He ushered me up into the attic of his old house and told me to lie down. Then he pressed his thumbs into my muscles. The pain shot deep into my body and I cried out. When I screamed, he said, "That's good. Scream all you want. It will help let out the tension." I accepted his invitation and allowed my pain to surge up from some hidden storehouse, screaming at the top of my lungs for the entire hour. I walked out feeling cleansed and free.

A few days later the fatigue started again. I went back to Peter and told him I still felt drained. "I must be sick," I said.

He knew exactly what was wrong. "You have low blood sugar. Most doctors don't even know it exists."

I returned to the clinic and told them about my condition. They said low blood sugar was extremely rare, and there was no reason to suspect I had it.

"Look," I said. "I'm sick and you have to find out what is wrong with me. You can't just leave me like this." They relented.

The morning of the test, I arrived on an empty stomach and drank a sweet, syrupy concoction. They took blood samples at regular intervals while I sat in the waiting room, agitated and afraid. While sitting there, I noticed I was feeling more alert than usual. *This is a waste of time. If I'm not tired during the exam, how are they going to see it on the blood test?*

A few days later, I met the internal medicine specialist, he in his short, combed hair and three-piece suit, and me in my big bushy hair and sideburns and my blue jeans with holes in the knees. Thumbing through my chart he said, "Don't you realize how much these tests cost? You've wasted a lot of our valuable resources." Tense with disgust, he referred me to a psychiatrist.

The medical doctors didn't know how to help me so they are foisting me off on a shrink. I hated the suggestion that it was "all in my mind," but since I didn't have any other options, I followed through.

When the psychiatrist welcomed me to his office, he moved his head in the disjointed manner of someone born blind. *Oh, great,* I thought. *How is this man going to help me if he can't even see?* I gave him an overview of my concerns. As I spoke, I heard the flat tone of my own voice. I felt like I was dead inside. He cheerfully suggested I take a more humorous view of life.

"Go to a movie. Laugh a little. Don't take everything so seriously." When he put his hand on my shoulder, I felt an electric stream of compassion. I instantly knew he cared about me. No one had expressed concern about me in months. No one even knew I existed, except for this blind man who let me know through his touch that I was not alone.

When the session ended, he handed me a prescription. I looked up the medication in the medical library. It was an anti-depressant. How ridiculous. There was nothing wrong with my mind. I threw the prescription in the trash. *God, these doctors have no idea how to help me.*

Since the clinic offered no further aid, I began to look for alternative approaches. The bookrack at the health food store provided a good source of information.

I picked out one book by Aldous Huxley, a writer I admired because his novel, *Brave New World,* offered a dark view of a sinister future. His was one of the first books that showed me how adults were screwing up the world. I was surprised to learn that Huxley also wrote a book about how to see without glasses. In *The Art of Seeing*, Huxley claimed that people don't need corrective lenses, and that in fact, eyeglasses cause near-sightedness. He claimed that if I took off my glasses, I could do simple eye exercises that would restore my vision. This made perfect sense. Glasses were a manmade concoction that obviously divided me from my natural self. Giving up my contact lenses seemed like a smart move.

The next day, I walked outside without lenses. The first few minutes were like a miracle. I looked up at the mountains above Berkeley, and everything looked crisp. I could see! I knew this was going to work. But later, when I tried to read, the page was a blur.

Huxley had provided vague instructions about eye exercises, but I couldn't translate them into a practical plan. For help, I went to the student eye clinic and told the optometrist I couldn't wear glasses anymore because I wanted to strengthen my eyes. He didn't understand what I was talking about.

"You mean you don't know about Huxley's system?" I asked, hoping he was at least curious.

"You have a simple choice," he said. "Either correct your vision with lenses or remain legally blind."

Another doctor leaving me stranded. I would have to solve my own problems. I decided to give Huxley's method more time. I could read at close range, and after a while my eyes would improve with exercise. For now, I would remain legally blind.

Despite my fatigue and blurred vision, I continued with my plan. When the school year started, I took a full load of science courses. As I had done throughout my college career, I aimed at extremely difficult courses, pushing myself to my limit, afraid that anything too easy would bore me. I signed up for courses that would fuel my desire to become a doctor, either by meeting the admission requirements or by contributing to my own deeper understanding of medicine.

I enrolled in a course on Medical Physics, because I loved both medicine and physics. It would be my one easy course. In the first lecture, the professor didn't bother to explain what the course was about. He immediately started writing equations on the board. From the few words he spoke while he was writing, I gathered these were meant to calculate the dosage of radiation in the body. I glanced around nervously. For the other students, this was a review. For me, it was an indication that things were going to be moving faster than I had expected. And to make matters worse, even when I sat on the front row, I could barely read the board.

I couldn't imagine going back to my contact lenses. That seemed like backsliding. Fortunately, I had an old pair of glasses that I kept for an emergency, and this was certainly an emergency. I hated wearing them, fearing they would weaken my eyes, but I needn't have worried about that. The last time I wore these glasses was in high school, and they were so far out of date that even with them on, everything was still a blur.

My microbiology course also turned out to be more advanced than I expected. In the first lecture, the professor told about breakthroughs in the understanding mitosis, the process during which a dividing cell makes two copies of its own genetic material. When I studied this in high school, no one could explain the mechanism by which the two halves of the chromosome separated. Since then, electron microscopes detected tiny cables called microtubules pulling the strands of DNA apart.

The professor scribbled formulas on the board to explain the chemical structure of these cables. I was fascinated by the new information, but horrified by my ignorance. I had never studied chemical interactions at this level of detail. I guessed from the questions asked by other students that they knew exactly what he was talking about. Their comfort level scared me. I could compete in a classroom where we all had similar backgrounds, but it sounded like these students were way ahead of me. My intellectual ambition had carried me into heights so rarified I was having trouble breathing.

I also signed up for organic chemistry, reputed to be one of the most difficult of all pre-med courses. Five years had passed since my last chemistry course, which was never my best subject, anyway. But if I was going to get into medical school, I had to overcome this hurdle. I arrived late to a lecture hall packed with more than a hundred ambitious pre-med students. From the back row, I could barely see the professor, who was introducing the history of organic chemistry.

"The first organic chemical that was ever synthesized was uric acid," he said, and the class tittered slightly.

How sad. Animals have been urinating since the beginning of time, and we humans are so proud of our ability to manufacture the same stuff in a lab.

Back in my tiny room, afraid, tired, and almost blind, I couldn't study for more than a few minutes at a time. By the end of the first week, I was completely out of touch with what the professors were teaching I tried to brush away the doubts, but there was no way I could ignore the growing certainty that I was losing my grip. I couldn't believe it. After working so hard to get back into school, my dream of becoming a doctor was slipping away.

If I stayed in school, I would certainly get F's, making an indelible blot on my already shady academic record. I faced the inevitable next step: I filed the paperwork to drop out.

Ever since high school, the only way I could visualize myself as an adult was as a doctor. Now, as I filled out the withdrawal form, each stroke of the pencil cut away another strand of the rope that linked me to my adult destiny. By the time I finished the form, the rope was cut, dropping me into an abyss.

In my exit interview with the dean of the engineering college, he looked at my transcript and said, "You're not even taking engineering courses." His face hardened. "You really don't belong here."

He was right. I only applied to the engineering school as a trick to take pre-med courses. *If I were in his shoes, I would despise me, too.* I walked out blind, starving, and friendless. What was I going to do?

Fortunately, the government came to my rescue. A community vo-tech school offered a free course to train people to become ironworkers. The availability of the course validated the hippie philosophy that there was plenty of abundance in society if only you knew where to look.

The class was held in an enclosed yard outside the school building. In late fall, the temperature had dropped low enough to require a flannel shirt. The teacher, a retired ironworker, told us we could make a good living in the construction industry. To qualify for entry-level positions, we had to learn all about rebar. These were long, thin bars of steel that were used to reinforce concrete. Our first task was to learn to tie bars together, using pliers and a spool of wire that we wore in dispensers on our belts.

He demonstrated it and then asked us to try it.

"Keep in mind that in order to qualify as ironworkers you need to move really fast".

I tried it a few times myself. It wasn't too hard, and I figured if this was all there was to ironworking, I would be fine. However, when he checked us with his stopwatch, I turned out to be the slowest one in the class. I hoped that with practice, I could catch up to the others.

Then he showed us how to hoist the long, heavy bars onto our shoulders.

"Pay attention to how I'm lifting these," he said. He made it look easy. "As apprentices, your main job will be to haul rebar up to the workmen. You're going to have to really hustle." When I tried to pick up three of the bars, my knees buckled. I was beginning to wonder if I would ever qualify for this work.

"And you'll need a good sense of balance," he continued. "Most of the jobs require you to carry bars across the girders in high-rise buildings, with nothing beneath you." This information shocked me. I had seen photos of workers walking on girders high up in buildings but I had no intention of ever becoming one. However, since I didn't know what else to do, I stuck around for the next lesson — welding.

The teacher stood next to the propane and oxygen tanks. When he turned the knobs, the gas made a delightful hissing sound as it escaped through the nozzle.

"Then ignite it with this lighter," he said, striking a spark.

There was an audible snap as the invisible gas sprung into flame. I loved that sound, and couldn't wait to try it myself.

He showed us how to use the flame to join two pieces of steel by creating a puddle of molten metal along the seam. After the puddle hardened, the two pieces had been joined into one.

I tried it, directing the flame at a piece of steel. As it melted, I became mesmerized by the brilliant oranges and yellows, with swirls of mysterious dark reds. The hues shifted too fast for me to follow, as if from this simple material an infinite variety of colors were emerging. I did it again and again.

I soon wanted to go beyond simply joining two pieces of steel. I experimented, cutting pieces of scrap into quirky shapes and then welding them together into abstract sculptures. Even though I had stopped smoking dope, I still managed to see the shapes of horses among the twisted chunks of metal.

My teacher stopped beside me. "What are you doing?"

"Don't you see the horse?" I asked, tracing the shape with my finger.

He looked upset. "This is what I hate. We need these materials, and you're wasting them."

I looked up at him, feeling sad. He seemed like a nice guy. I couldn't understand why he was being so uptight.

By the end of the class it was clear I was never going to be strong enough, fast enough, or brave enough to be an ironworker. I heard that some of the hippies were receiving food stamps, and since I had no income I was accepted into the program.

Searching for a Heart of Gold

With no hope of going back to school, no friends, and no particular reason for living, my longing for Patricia increased until it felt like a scream deep in my soul. My heart hurt. My skin hurt. The air around me hurt. I sobbed alone in my room. When I slunk around Berkeley, I was terrified that if I saw her, I wouldn't be able to handle the avalanche of feelings.

A few months after we broke up, I wrote her a note asking if we could talk. I was the one who left, but perhaps she would take me back. She wrote saying she would meet me on campus.

When I saw her, I thought her smile would drive me mad. Love surged through me in great torrents. I wanted to be around her all the time. But after a warm greeting and hug, she pulled away, no longer smiling. Avoiding my eyes, she said she missed me but she was with a new guy, Steve.

She was so beautiful, but instead of sitting together basking in each other's love, she was reciting our death sentence. Steve was her husband's best friend. In high school, the three of them were inseparable. When her husband was killed in Vietnam, she and Steve mourned together. After I'd left her last year, Steve came through again. He wanted to marry her and help her take care of her baby.

I was heartsick as she spelled out the morbid details that would forever exclude me from her life. During her explanation she looked down, and then she grew quiet and started to tremble. "I'm so sorry," she said, finally looking at me. "I can't stay."

She pulled back from our final embrace, looked desperately into my eyes, and walked away. I knew she was doing the best thing for herself and for her child, but that didn't stop the onslaught of pain that engulfed me.

I thought I was going to be a doctor. I wanted to understand the mysteries of the material universe. I wanted to stop war. I wanted a girl. Now it was all out of reach. I had nothing. The California sunshine seemed a sham. All around me were young people, growing and learning.

But I was not one of them.

§§§

In the fall, during the first downpour of Berkeley's wet season, the wind blew hard against my makeshift cabin and water started leaking into the room. I raced against the puddles, moving my stuff so it wouldn't be ruined. After the storm, I continued to feel vulnerable, desperately looking for a way to restore my little home to safety. When the couple who rented the main house offered no solution, I realized I had to solve this problem myself.

Next to the garage, on the other side of a fence, a hippie worked quietly, hoeing and weeding his garden. I envied his purposeful, daily routine. He seemed to know who he was and what he was supposed to do.

I leaned over to the fence. "Can you give me some advice?"

"Sure, man," he said.

"My roof is leaking."

He came over with a ladder and we climbed up on the top of the old garage and examined the tarpaper roof. He said that it wasn't that hard to fix. Just cover it with a layer of fresh paper and seal it with melted tar. He could loan me a hotplate.

I went to a hardware store and bought a block of tar but the tarpaper was expensive. I knew there were always roofing materials at construction sites around the university. I took advantage of the university's abundance by helping myself to a roll of tarpaper and walked home with it on my shoulder, heart racing and hoping no one would stop me. The paper was nowhere near as heavy as the steel bars I had to carry in ironworking class.

Before the next storm, I hauled my equipment up onto the roof, chipped a block of tar into a pot, melted it, and then slathered the hot tar onto the paper. The resulting dry ceiling restored my sense of safety, bringing with it pride that I had moved beyond book learning. Solving a problem in the real world gave me hope that I could learn to become a working man after all. When I saw my neighbor, I thanked him for his help.

"Good going, man," he said. "Hey, we're having a few people over for dinner Saturday. Why don't you come?" I had been so alone for so long, I forgot what it was like to be around people. I said "sure," hoping I would feel OK in their company.

When I arrived, a young woman greeted me. She had long, light-brown hair and was dressed in overalls, just like her man. The living room was furnished with mattresses on the floor. It looked warm and inviting.

I tried to enjoy myself, but I felt so lost. After dinner, leaning on cushions, I focused on the music, hoping for answers to lead me out of my dead end. Neil Young's album dropped onto the turntable, and he began to sing about his search for someone with a heart of gold. His plaintive cry filled me. I, too, was on that search. Patricia had a heart of gold, but that didn't work out.

Her image, combined with Neil Young's song, reawakened pain that radiated from my heart to every molecule in my body. I wondered if there was another person out there who could help me find my way. I went home in the dark, lay down on my bed, and cried.

§§§

With nothing else to do, I walked around Berkeley looking at people, hoping each one might give me a tiny spark of life, so that if I passed enough of them I would feel truly alive. On one of these walks, I saw an announcement for a lecture by Jane Goodall, a famous anthropologist who had lived with a colony of chimpanzees in Africa. I had long been curious about the fact that when you strip away the trappings of civilization, humans are a type of primate. To learn more about my true nature, I attended the lecture.

When Goodall walked to the podium, I was struck by her command of the stage and passion about her topic. I wanted to follow this woman, whose brilliance shone like a beacon in the dimness of my existence.

She spoke about the animals she had been observing by name, as if they were her children or close friends. Their quirks and simple lifestyle fascinated me. Their behavior was dictated not by complex ideas but by their innate nature.

It was obvious to me that they were the true people and we civilized ones were the fakes, constantly bumbling and inventing our way forward. Over the last few hundred years, our so-called progress had resulted in misery and destruction. The lecture convinced me that to find my authentic self, I needed to live more like the chimpanzees.

One way to live more like chimpanzees would be to eat a more natural diet. At the health food store I found a book by Arnold Ehret in which he claimed that all illness is due to cooked food, and that we can find all the nutrition we need in raw foods. His idea resonated with my belief that I was suffering from civilization. Chimpanzees don't cook, so why should we?

Ehret suggested that for an initial cleansing diet, you should only eat grapes. I followed his advice, consuming them by the pound. The first couple of days I felt as if I were floating. Over the following weeks, though, the lightness turned into dizziness, and my interest in food grew to an obsession. I filled grocery bags with grapes, and when even that quantity didn't satisfy me, I expanded my diet to include grapefruits and oranges. For an hour or two after I stuffed myself with fruit, I felt too bloated to consider eating anything else. But soon I was hungry again. The only time I wasn't thinking about food was when I slept, so I slept more and more.

To alleviate my growing hunger, I added other foods, such as raw cashew butter, avocadoes, raisins, and dates. I wasn't sure if chimpanzees ate these foods, but at least they were raw. Yet no matter how much I ate, I couldn't find peace. I envied the chimpanzees. With the vast variety of the forest at their disposal, they could eat exactly what they needed.

On one of my forays to the health food store, I found a new way to solve my problems in a book by Wilhelm Reich, a famous colleague of Sigmund Freud. The book was about "Orgone energy," which the author claimed was the essence of life. Apparently this subtle, powerful force had something to do with orgasms. I liked the idea that orgasms were the most important thing in the universe.

Squinting and reading a few paragraphs at a time, I struggled to make sense of his idea. It seemed to fit in with my search for a pure, natural self. In the wild, without the interference of civilization, animals must have a perfect relationship with their sexuality. But his ideas were more complicated than simply having perfect sex. Orgone energy was cosmic. It controlled not only the power within a person but also in the material world. He was able to somehow harness this same energy to make rain, and he developed a system that cured cancer by focusing energy in pyramid-shaped boxes.

Perhaps Orgone energy would heal my fatigue and get me back on track. I didn't have a pyramid-shaped box, but perhaps I could invent my own way of stirring up the energy. I struck on the idea that I might be able to tap into it with pure, free dancing. I loved the cosmic sense of freedom I achieved when I let my body merge with music. Surely if there was a life force trapped inside me, I could release it by dancing.

Alone in my room, I turned on the music and felt my body get lost in the rhythm. I leapt and weaved, undulating my legs and arms, bobbing my head and torso, in time with the many beats I found inside the music. I danced for hours desperately attempting to make the Orgone energy flow through me. My waves of fatigue bordered on despair, yet I kept moving, hoping that this was the pathway to freedom. However, my method didn't help.

Reich's book was abstract. I hoped to find more specific instructions about how he had awakened this energy but the only other book I could find by him was a small volume titled *Listen, Little Man!* I bought it, hoping it would give me insights about how to save myself. It turned out that Reich had been sent to prison for claiming to have discovered an alternative way of curing cancer. His book *Listen, Little Man!* was a bitter diatribe against everyone too small-minded to understand his great ideas. Reich said that anyone could have tried his ideas and seen for themselves how powerful they were, but instead they wanted to destroy him. I shared his bitterness. That was how I was beginning to feel too, furious with society for trapping me in this losing battle with my mind. If I couldn't figure out how to get out of it soon, I would go crazy.

The Perfect Escape

I walked around Berkeley all day, searching for the meaning of my life, but found little pleasure in the passing faces, since I could barely see them. By evening, exhausted and ready to give up for the day, I walked the few blocks to the garage I called home. I opened the door to find a woman sitting in the dim light.

She stood up and smiled but I couldn't make out who she was. She greeted me by name and reached out to hug me. Just as the baby in her arms began to wail, I exclaimed, "Roberta!" She was one of the few women at the University of Wisconsin with whom I could converse like a friend.

I hadn't heard from her since I arrived in California almost two years earlier. Roberta ... here now ... with a baby. ... I tried to be welcoming, despite the fact that I just wanted to sleep.

"How did you find me?" I asked.

"I asked around in Madison and Jason gave me your address," she said, her voice somewhat disembodied in the dim light.

I knew Jason had moved back to Madison, but I had not heard from him in months. "I don't recall you being friends with Jason."

"Yes, he's working at a supermarket stocking the produce section."

I thought about this for a moment. Jason was back in Madison, and Roberta knew him. It was like a conspiracy of friendship. I didn't even know I had any friends.

"You have a baby now," I said, raising my voice to be heard above his cries.

She told me her son had hemophilia, so if he received even a minor bruise he could bleed to death. I looked at his tiny form and couldn't blame him for screaming. He had a hard road ahead.

"I moved to Costa Rica to live on the beach where he can play on the soft sand. There is a whole community of us down there."

Pointing at a book sitting by my bed, she said, "I see you are reading about diet."

I told her about my fruit diet and how I had stopped wearing my glasses in order to live unencumbered by civilization.

"Why don't you come down and live with me on the beach? I pick all the fruit I want right off the trees."

Hope flickered in my mind. This could be my chance to live like a chimpanzee. Roberta seemed like a messenger, guiding me to my ideal life. But my excitement was smothered by a blanket of fatigue and depression. I asked Roberta if she was going to be around town much longer.

"No, I'm just passing through."

"I'd like to join you on the beach. But right now, I have to sleep."

She gave me instructions on how to reach her. We hugged, and she left.

Now, finally, I had a purpose. All I had to do was raise the money for the plane ticket. I had some money left in the bank from my college loan, and I would sell the textbooks and records I had brought with me from college.

Jerry Waxler

I placed my boxes on the sidewalk in front of the house, and watched passersby thumb through my college treasures, my copy of Herbert Marcuse's *One Dimensional Man*, Marshall McLuhan's *The Medium is the Message*, my collection of existential novels, and science textbooks. My records were up for sale too — The Beatles, Dylan, Beethoven, Coltrane. As each one disappeared, a piece of my past went with it.

When the sale was finished, I had no more stuff to keep me in Berkeley, and I had just enough money for a ticket to Central America. After that, I would live on the beach and eat fruit from the trees.

I wrote to Roberta, telling her I was ready. While I waited for her response, I spotted an announcement for a yoga class. I knew hardly anything about yoga. It had always seemed too disconnected from reality for my analytical mind. But now that my world had unraveled, I decided there was little to lose.

The class was held in a dimly lit school gymnasium with hardwood floors and no furniture. I found a place among the people seated on mats, facing a man at the front of the room. He wore a turban and tunic, had a long beard, and when he spoke, his voice was calm, almost reverential. He quietly instructed us to stretch out, to close our eyes, to breathe deeply, let all the tension go. Through various postures and instructions, he showed us how to look within ourselves for peace.

These instructions to look within my own mind seemed perfect. My outer life had completely collapsed and all that remained was the activity inside my own mind. Now this teacher was giving me ideas about how to quiet my thoughts. I felt grateful to him for this gift.

He told us that for thousands of years, people had used these postures and meditation practices in order to understand the mind. Guided by this helpful man, surrounded by people who wanted to find inner peace, I felt a calm satisfaction, different from anything I ever experienced.

Until this point, I always assumed knowledge needed to be verified scientifically. The peace I experienced during that hour made me wonder if this type of wisdom might help me find deeper truths.

After the meeting, I lingered, trying to delay the emotional chaos waiting for me in my room. I even overcame my shyness to speak to an attractive girl. "Excuse me," I said. She turned toward me and smiled.

"There's one thing that puzzles me about this class." I felt a wave of gratitude to actually be speaking to another person. "What did the instructor mean when he said, 'If anything happens that confuses you, please raise your hand and someone will come over to talk about it?'"

"Well, I can tell you a story about that. A friend of mine attended this same yoga class a few weeks ago. She closed her eyes and started to hear a loud ringing sound throughout the room. She assumed the teacher had wheeled out a gong and was playing it. But when she opened her eyes, she found herself lying on the mat. Everyone else had moved on to a different exercise and no musical instrument was in sight."

"So she lost track of time?" I said.

"Exactly. My friend didn't understand what was happening and she asked the yoga teacher what it meant. He told her, "You know in the Bible where it says, 'In the beginning was the Word, and the Word was God.' That gong sound you heard is the Word."

Could it be true? This was the first time I had ever heard of a link between the Bible and yoga. I wondered what other mysteries might be hiding in these ancient teachings.

We chatted a little longer and it turned out the girl with whom I was speaking had attended college in Madison. There it was — Madison again! The place kept calling to me. I even had a recurring dream in which I was walking, walking, endlessly walking through the streets of Madison alone, not knowing where I was going. And since I didn't know where I was going, I could never get there.

The Longest Day

Traveling from Berkeley to Madison, 1971

Ever since Roberta told me she bumped into Jason in Madison, I had been thinking about him. We seemed to have some sort of magical connection. He was the one person I wanted to see when I first arrived in California. And now that I was leaving California forever, I felt drawn to see him one last time. It seemed crazy to travel 2,000 miles just to say goodbye, but I couldn't shake the feeling that it was important.

On a sunny day in March of 1971, I threw a change of clothes in a small backpack, walked to the highway and held up a sign that said "Madison, Wisconsin." After a few hours of watching cars whiz by, I surrendered to hunger. Still holding my sign out toward the oncoming traffic, I turned and started walking back to my cabin, when a Volkswagen van pulled up alongside me. A clean-cut young man leaned out of the window. "Hop in. I'm going to Illinois. That'll get you 1,800 miles down the road."

Wow. I couldn't believe my luck. I told him I was unable to drive because of my eyesight, so on the way out of town he picked up another longhaired hitchhiker to share the driving. Then we started on the journey east.

I sat in the back seat, drifting in and out of sleep, listening to the owner and hitchhiker chatting. A thousand miles inland, we were climbing into the mountains. I was napping in the backseat when I heard shouting. I woke to see the van veering toward the edge of the road. There was no fence, and the shoulder dropped off so steeply I couldn't see the ground beyond it. The hitchhiker was behind the wheel, and the owner screamed, "Stop!" The driver screamed, "I can't!"

We were sliding sideways, as if a giant hand was pushing us toward the precipice. Then the van tipped. "We're going over!"

I reached up to brace myself against the ceiling as we flipped over, and then picked up speed as if we were going to flip again. I was just starting to grasp the enormity of the danger when we came to a stop.

Climbing out a broken window from the upside-down vehicle, I emerged into the icy wind. The other two guys emerged from the front, shaken but apparently OK. The three of us stood shivering on this barren mountainside, staring at the wreck.

"What happened?" I asked.

"The road was icy. A gust must have blown us off."

"I'm so sorry," the hippie said.

I looked up the embankment to see how far we had rolled. Thank God the hill leveled out. If it had been steeper or farther, I might not be standing here.

"What now?" I asked.

On the road above us, a truck had pulled over.

"He'll call for help, right?"

Too dazed to consider climbing up the steep incline, I just stood there. My only protection from the icy wind was the light jacket I had worn when I left balmy Berkeley. The pain from my cheeks, fingers, and ears built to a crescendo, as I silently screamed, wondering how much more of this bitter cold I could take. Then, a police car parked on the road above. The officer clambered down to us. Friendly and concerned, he offered us a ride into town. Once again my anger at the police was replaced by gratitude.

He took us to the local auto repair shop and we huddled in the overheated office while the owner of the vehicle talked to the shop owner. I tried to figure out what to do next. The accident didn't bother me; I didn't have much to live for anyway. But I couldn't just stay in this town.

"Where are we?" I asked the guy at the garage.

"Laramie, Wyoming."

I decided to use some of the money I was saving for Costa Rica. The policeman offered me a ride to the airport. I said goodbye and continued my journey by air.

§§§

That evening I reached Jason's apartment. After a warm hug, we sat across from each other at the kitchen table. Soft-spoken and gentle as usual, he was in one of his bearded phases. I told him about the changes I'd been going through and my plan to move to Central America. I was so caught up in my story that it took me a few minutes to realize he was barely paying attention.

"So what's going on with you?" I finally asked.

He leaned across the table and said in a serious tone, "I found a new master."

I had no idea what he meant. "What is a master?"

"We can talk about it tomorrow. Here. Read this," he said, handing me a book. I wasn't sure if I would be able to read all of that without glasses, but I took it, partly from politeness and partly from curiosity about what he was into.

He showed me the unfurnished guest room where I would be sleeping. On the floor, a few blankets would serve as my bed. We said goodnight, and he left me alone. How strange to be back in an apartment in Madison. When I left this town two springs ago, I was looking for my future in California. Now, after that catastrophic failure, here I was back again, still looking for my next step.

I lay on the floor propped up on an elbow, and opened the book, *The Living Master* by Katherine Windress, to the page Jason had bookmarked. The chapter was titled "Satsang in the Rose Garden." Holding the book close to my face, I began to read about a lovely garden in India where a guru was explaining his teachings to a few Western followers.

"Every individual is a drop in the ocean of God's love, and we want desperately to return to that ocean," he said. "Even though our soul wants to return to God, our mind attempts to satisfy its longing by dashing out into the world, acquiring things or looking for pleasure."

The utterly simple explanation gave me a glimmer of hope that I might be able to understand the misery I had been experiencing over the last couple of years. I kept reading.

"But no matter what we achieve, in each birth we accumulate more desires than we have fulfilled. These longings pull us back to the world to take another birth."

I had vaguely heard about this notion of reincarnation, but never took it seriously. However, reading it in these terms, as a way of explaining the journey of the soul, it made perfect sense.

"Through eons, we travel from birth to birth, sometimes born in a higher form, like a human or even higher, to etheric realms, and sometimes descending the wheel and going back down into a species of animal. Around and around we go, sometimes up, and sometimes down, but never reaching our destination. Eventually we grow weary of endless attempts to fulfill our desires. This longing to return to God is just the first step. We have been immersed in creation for so many lifetimes, we are trapped in it. To escape the wheel of reincarnation, we need the help of a living master to penetrate the illusion and return home."

Reincarnation? Masters? The soul? I never thought about any of these topics, but now, in this room, reading this book, on this night, it all made perfect sense. I let go of my preconceptions, and kept reading, as if I was finally finding the key to everything I had been seeking my whole life.

Perhaps I accepted this explanation because the scene in India felt so intimate, as though I was sitting there with those disciples in a beautiful garden. They looked to him as a selfless guide whose only motive was to serve them. Their love for him jumped from the pages and into my heart. I wanted him to tell me more.

Despite his simple language, he answered my deepest questions. He even answered questions I had never thought to ask. I had certainly never thought about a living master. I didn't even know such a concept existed, but now, in his presence in the pages of the book, it made perfect sense. Of course God would send a messenger in every age. How could it be any other way?

In my teens, I turned away from religion, expecting that school would teach me everything I needed. After years of study, attempting to absorb the thinking of the greatest minds of our age, I felt worse off than when I started. Now, in this humble room, reading a book about a man in India, I was learning how to tie it all together. As if a giant curtain had lifted, I could see the longings that created and sustained the world.

Then, Maharaj Ji said something that convinced me that this was the path I needed to follow. He said that God manifests Himself within each of us as an Audible Life Stream. Until we attune ourselves to God's presence, we only hear the noise of the world. By meditating, we would be able to hear the inner harmony.

This was the second time I had heard someone suggest that I could hear God. The first time had been just a week earlier when the girl in Berkeley, who happened to be from Madison, told me that the gong sound was the "logos" or the "word of God" mentioned in the Bible. Now, I was reading the same teaching. This insane, unbelievable coincidence only seemed possible if it was set in motion by the guiding hand of an invisible author.

Yesterday morning I was walking down to the highway in Berkeley with nothing to live for but fruit. Now, as I drifted off to sleep in Madison, I imagined sitting at the feet of a master, learning how to return the drop of my soul to the ocean of God's love.

Learning the Path

The next morning, Jason and I sat at the kitchen table again. This time, I was on fire with curiosity.

"Who is Maharaj Ji?" I asked.

Jason left briefly and brought back a photo of a man with a long beard and wearing turban.

"Have you met him?" I asked.

"No," he said. "I just missed his last visit to the States. I hope someday to be able to visit his spiritual center in India."

"How have you been learning about all of this?"

"A woman in town follows him. She's been loaning me books."

"I'm fascinated by this whole teaching, Jason. The wheel of reincarnation," I said, listening to the sound of that phrase. "I never thought about anything like that before, but as soon as he explained it, the whole cycle of life and death made sense."

"It helps me a lot," Jason said. "I could never understand how God would give us just one chance. Reincarnation means we can try over and over and over. It also helps me with forgiveness."

"Really? How so?"

"If someone is rude to me, instead of being upset about how unfair it is, I stop and think about all our past lifetimes, and how I was probably rude to him in another birth and now he's just paying me back."

"Neat," I said, practically shouting with excitement. "I love trying to understand the causes of things. This gives me a whole new language to help me explain what I'm going through."

"It's not as if we can actually see our past lives," he said. "There are millions of them and it would be a waste of energy to try to learn the details. But I find the general principle really helpful. Maharaj Ji uses the expression 'as you sow, so shall you reap.' Whatever you don't fulfill in one birth is added to the pile of things you have to pay back in the next."

Every answer brought up new questions. "Who are these teachers who are supposed to help us? Is there more than one?"

"There is always at least one living teacher on earth to guide home those who are ready."

"But why are they so hard to find?" I asked, thinking back to all the dead ends I had followed in my life.

"The message is always available, but people are so committed to what they already believe that they often persecute or even kill those who deliver this message. They are far more tolerant of dead teachers than living ones."

"Ouch!" I said. "That's crazy!"

"Yes," Jason added. "It's so hard to find a teacher, and yet when we're ready, one appears. At least that was the way it worked for me. And it sounds like it's working that way for you, too."

"All this time I've been looking to science for answers, and despite all my intense efforts to understand the material world, my reason for living has been draining away. I'm so glad I found this."

We sat in silence. I wanted to celebrate my good fortune, but my mind kept racing to the next question.

"Journey of the soul. ... I never even thought about my soul. Now I realize it's on a journey, and I keep taking births over and over until I get it right."

Jason paused to think about what I said, giving me time to relax and prepare to listen. When he spoke, it was worth the wait.

"You don't get off the wheel of reincarnation just because you figured it all out. In fact, lots of people think they have figured it out. They feel proud and admire their own achievements. They begin to long for all the pleasures they have been denying themselves. Their discipline slips. Once they're on the downward slide, they forget their wisdom and have to go around the wheel again."

I tried to picture some soul who had reached a high birth, perhaps a prince, or even a holy man, thinking they were on top of creation, and then for some reason they slipped and plummeted back down to lower species. "That would feel like a nightmare, watching yourself pulled down from the pinnacle like that."

I thought for a bit longer and started to laugh. "Wait a minute. I guess I can imagine it perfectly. In fact, I experienced it myself. I was sure I was going to be a doctor and nothing could stop me. Then, bit by bit, my mind tricked me into thinking that I could find true happiness by heading in the other direction. Within just a few years, instead of trying to be a doctor, I was trying to live like a chimpanzee. I really thought that was the right way to go. I lived through the very process you are describing. I was falling to a lower species, not within thousands of births, but within one."

Jason said, "You must have been around that wheel a million times. God decided to pick this time to send someone to guide you home."

I thought how God had intervened in my destiny. I had been actively pursuing my new ambition to live like a chimpanzee, and just as I prepared to go to the forest, I followed the impulse to visit Jason. Where did that impulse come from? If I had not followed it, I would be heading across the border right now. God must have had a hand in this detour.

I looked around the apartment. I had lived in many such places during my years in Madison. During that period, I was constantly on fire, unsure of who I was and where I was going. Now, everything was different. Despite the beat up furniture and the dreary winter light, I felt as if this was the inner sanctum of the holiest temple. It occurred to me that this was the most peaceful I had felt in Madison since the day I arrived.

Turning Away from the Abyss

Jason looked at the clock and said, "I'm sorry to cut this off. I have to go to work for a few hours. Why don't you read more of the book and we'll talk when I get back." After he left, I looked around the old apartment. It reminded me of all the apartments I had lived in during my college years—dingy, with old, used furniture. But I was no longer a student. I wasn't sure what I was. Perhaps a refugee?

I opened Katherine Windress's book again and started from the beginning. She told about her own journey to find meaning in her life, and how she had burned out all her options. Her story sounded like mine. She had reached the end of her road, and then found a book in the bookstore. She read it in a blaze of curiosity. To learn more, she wrote a letter to an address listed in the back of the book. That started a process that resulted in her trip to India to meet her master. When she finally met her spiritual teacher, her devotion was electric. Driven almost crazy with her passion to meet God, she stared at her master as if her love would open the doors and reveal the secrets promised by this path.

For years, I too had been driven by profound questions, first trying to find the answers in science, and then in social philosophy, and no matter how deeply I went into those topics, I was never able to quench my thirst. Now, thanks to this author's journey to India, I discovered answers in an entirely unexpected direction. Until a few days ago, I didn't even know my questions were spiritual. I only knew that if I didn't find a way to visualize my place in the world, I would go mad.

Despite the fact that the answers in the book were different from anything I had read or thought about before, they felt instantly satisfying, as if my mind was prepared in advance for this exact explanation. It all fit together, combining ancient ideas like yoga and mysticism into a form that I could grasp with my scientifically oriented thinking.

Katherine's teacher even described the teachings as "the science of the soul," because when you practice meditation, you explore truth within the laboratory of your own mind. This promise of direct observation satisfied my thirst for proof. Of course, in the beginning, I would need to trust these teachers. Then, over time, I would be able to see for myself, not after I died but while I was living. The more I studied, the clearer I was that I needed to follow this path.

When I heard Jason open the door, I barely gave him enough time to take off his jacket.

"Tell me more about the soul," I begged.

He laughed. "I see you want to know everything all at once. That's the way I was when I found the Path. Let me make us some tea."

While the water boiled he puttered around the kitchen, peacefully preparing the cups. His methodical movements helped me regain my poise. When he finally set my cup on the table in front of me, its warmth and the waft of the herb comforted me. I was eager to listen to every word.

"Maharaj Ji uses the analogy of a thousand pitchers of water. Each one reflects the light from the sun, but there is only one sun.

That's the way the soul is. Each of us contains a reflection of God. And to become whole, each of us longs to return to Him."

"What a beautiful image," I said. "So how do we get back?"

"Meditate, meditate, meditate," he laughed.

"I've heard of meditation but I don't know anything about it."

"That's one of the key points to the teaching. To grow closer to God, you have to still your mind. When you're initiated, you receive a mantra that you must repeat mentally while keeping your attention at the eye center," he said, pointing to a spot on his forehead between his eyes.

"That sounds easy."

Jason smiled. "It does sound easy, but it's a very long process. At first, you spend a lot of time wrestling with all the thoughts that pop into your head, like planning the next meal or worrying about an argument. Those worries are a lot more persistent than you realize."

"So how long will it take me to calm my mind?"

"We're not supposed to think about a time limit. We just keep trying. It's the relentless effort that gradually pulls us up toward God."

"I'm desperate, Jason. I'm going to work really hard."

"The longing for progress is wonderful. But pace yourself. It could take lifetimes. There's an old yogi saying. 'If you told me you could move a mountain with your mental powers, I would believe you. But I have never yet met anyone who can control his own mind.' In other words, you can't rise above your own mind. Your mind will always win." We both laughed at the irony.

"The mind has had a free run for millions of lifetimes, going wherever it pleases. Now that we're on the path, we work hard to reel it back in. In addition to the daily meditation, he also recommends we repeat the mantra every chance we get. My job at a supermarket requires hardly any mental effort, and gives me the freedom to repeat my mantra all day."

"That's interesting. The thing I hate most about boring jobs is that I never know what to do with my mind."

"Now you'll have something to do." Jason laughed. "But not all of Maharaj Ji's initiates have menial jobs. There are lawyers and doctors on the Path, too. I can't figure out how they do it, but it appears to be possible."

I was so excited, I stood and paced around the room. I was learning about the nature of my soul, as well as a system that would help me fulfill longings I had never even noticed. Returning to God was exactly what I wanted to do.

"So what do I have to do to join?"

"You have to agree to follow the four vows."

"What are they?"

"The first one is to meditate for two and a half hours a day. That's the key to everything. Maharaj Ji says it's like tithing your time. Two and a half hours is about ten percent of your day."

"OK. I can do that."

"You have to be vegetarian. No meat, poultry, fish, or eggs."

"That's easy," I said. "You started teaching me about being vegetarian the first day I showed up at your place in California." That seemed like a lifetime ago. It was hard to believe it was less than two years.

Jason smiled. "Back then, we avoided meat for a whole list of reasons. The Path adds one I never knew about: When you eat flesh, you absorb the karma of the animal. Their load is added to yours, weighing you down and making it harder to return to God."

"OK. If he says those things are bad for your soul, then I'll never eat them again. What else?"

"You have to stop taking drugs and alcohol. They scatter your mind out into the world."

"I've been so spaced out the last few months, I stopped using marijuana, so that's no problem. And I've never been into alcohol. I vow it. What else?"

"For some people, this is the hardest one of all." He paused, and I wondered why he was looking so serious. "You have to live a moral life. That means no sex out of wedlock." I sighed, feeling a mixture of relief and sorrow.

"I can see that might be a problem for some people, Jason, but not for me. I'm not doing well in that department. This doesn't even require a change. I'm already obeying it."

I was excited to realize there was nothing standing in my way. This was my new life, my new path.

"I want this, Jason. This is exactly what I've been looking for. I want a truth I can see for myself. What about money?" I asked. "How much does it cost?"

"There's no charge."

I felt relieved again. "That's good. Because all I have left is what I've scraped together for my plane ticket. So what's the next step?"

"You apply and Maharaj Ji decides if you are ready."

"What do you mean, 'if I'm ready?' I *am* ready."

"That's his call," Jason said.

It sounded like a mere formality. Of course he would say yes. But what if he said no? I couldn't let myself think about that. I had to forge ahead. Jason said he would get an application for me, and he would list himself as my sponsor.

I thought about the sudden turn my life had taken. When I first arrived in Madison two days ago, the world had seemed dim and hopeless. In my desperation, I had seen eating fruit from trees as the ultimate calling of my life. Now, I had something to live for. This Path offered me light, and my whole body was crying out for it. I would do whatever was necessary to follow this philosophy.

Returning to the World

When I needed a break from reading, sleeping and meditating, I went out walking on campus, through streets I had walked a thousand times. During the years I had been a student here, I longed to feel part of the crowd, and no matter how many times I failed, I kept hoping that if I could just say the right things, my fellow students would magically embrace me. Now, after two disastrous years in Berkeley and my newfound spiritual direction, I walked among them feeling invisible—an old, blind man heading in a new direction.

But what exactly was my new direction? I knew what I had to do to satisfy my soul. I needed to meditate and follow the Path. But how was I supposed to live in the world? After years of believing in nothing, I felt like I had walked up to the edge of a cliff and, despite my new philosophy, I was still teetering at the edge.

I returned to the apartment to read more, hoping Maharaj Ji's advice would help me find my way back to solid ground. In several passages, Maharaj Ji made it clear that the Path was for "householders," meaning people who raise families. Since I didn't have a family, I wasn't sure how this applied to me.

When Jason returned from work, I asked him what he thought about my plans to move to Central America to eat fruit from the trees.

"Your karmas and intuitions will lead you where you need to go."

"But what do you think Maharaj Ji would say?"

Jason smiled. "All the hippies wrestle with similar problems, hoping to avoid the complication of needing a job. Maharaj Ji says that doing your duty is part of life, and that the spiritual path is not an excuse to escape responsibility."

Over the next few days, I began to accept the fact that I had to take responsibility for myself. And since I was here in Madison, the first obvious step toward that goal would be to complete my college degree. But how would that be possible? I was almost blind and my mind was so foggy. I doubted I could pass even one of my incomplete courses. It would be miraculous if I could finish all three. But Maharaj Ji said to do our best, and leave the rest to God, so I started to line up the material I would need.

One task I needed to complete was the essay about Marshall McLuhan's futuristic idea that the world was becoming a global village. I met with the professor and gave him the drafted paper that I had already prepared. With some pleading, I convinced him to pass me.

My notes about General Relativity were in worse shape. When I tried to imagine what I would say to the professor, I reflected on how the Path had shown me physics in a new light.

Twentieth century physicists had discovered outrageous contradictions: that you could change the outcome of an experiment as soon as you observed it; that particles are really clouds of probability; that energy can be borrowed from some invisible, infinite well and then paid back a millionth of a second later. These discoveries contradicted all the logic and rationality that science had been building up for centuries.

Those twentieth-century scientists drilled deeper and deeper into material reality, and now I understood why they could never get all the way to the bottom. Material reality was one big illusion. No wonder my physics classes had seemed increasingly bizarre.

Even though these equations would never provide ultimate truth, I still needed to pass my course. I met with the professor and explained my situation, and convinced him that the work that I had done was worthy of a grade. He too agreed to let me pass.

Now my degree was in the hands of the professor of my Statistical Thermodynamics course. I set up an appointment with him, hoping to convince him that despite my inability to solve the equations, at least I had a good grasp of the basic principles.

During our meeting, when he wrote an equation on the board, I leaned close and squinted. I stammered, trying to repeat the things I knew. Finally, he said he would pass me. I couldn't see the equations, but I could easily see the compassion in his eyes. My gratitude poured out in a flood of relief. I earned my college degree, gasping and crawling across the finish line.

Now what? I was still a wreck and didn't know where to be or what to do. Living on the beach no longer sounded appropriate.

I kept meditating and reading the books, hoping for guidance. In one of the question-and-answer sessions, a Westerner said to Maharaj Ji, "My parents hate my lifestyle, and I feel like I have to stay away from them. I know the Path is all about love, but I don't understand how to love them."

"You can't run away from your responsibility to your family," he answered. "You were born into their care. Now do your duty to them." Several Westerners asked similar questions about their relationship to their family. His message was consistent. "Do your duty."

My decision to move to Central America had only been to serve myself. Now, I was going to need to think about my parents. How had I missed this before? Even the Ten Commandments included honoring my father and mother. But that was just some old religious dogma that never made any sense. Hearing it from my spiritual teacher was different.

Since I had never considered my duty to my parents, I didn't know what it meant or where to start. After days of thinking about my options, I decided I would need to move closer to them.

My life in California had already come to an end. I had sold everything. Now, instead of moving to the jungle, I would move east to Philadelphia, to live near my parents and do my duty to them. Even though I didn't know how to serve them, I hoped my new Path would help me understand.

Back To the East Coast

Philadelphia, 1971

The last time I was in Philadelphia, a couple of years earlier, my parents still lived in the row home where I grew up. Since then they had moved to a new high-rise complex adjoining a golf course. As I approached, a doorman courteously asked me to sign the guestbook. Then he phoned upstairs to tell my parents their son was here. "Yes, Mrs. Waxler," he said and waved me in.

A doorman? How peculiar. This man had to approve my visit. Even though their new apartment was just a couple of miles away from the row home where I grew up, it seemed like a different world.

I was different, too. I had shaved off the sideburns that had signified my countercultural rebellion. In fact, I had completely reversed my thinking about my parents. I could barely even remember why I had been angry with them. But despite this newfound acceptance, I was still unsure of how I would talk to them. I certainly couldn't explain my new beliefs.

When visiting them I would be attempting to keep at least part of my attention on meditation. I hoped my split focus wouldn't make me seem too weird.

The elevator arrived at their floor and I walked down the hall. As I passed each door, I noticed a Mezuzah affixed to the doorpost, confirming my guess that many of their Jewish neighbors had also moved into this building. The smell of cooked food varied as I made my way down the hall, until I arrived at 803, and knocked.

My parents opened the door, and we smiled and greeted each other. Dad shook my hand and Mom gave me a kiss. The moment I crossed the threshold, Mom offered me something to eat.

I grimaced, knowing she wouldn't understand my diet. "No thanks. How about a cup of tea?"

She looked disappointed. While I waited for the water to boil, I felt my chest tightening.

I walked over to the window and looked out over the lovely green golf course. "Do you mind if I open this?" I asked. "I need some fresh air."

"We've never opened it before," Dad said.

"We could check with the maintenance person tomorrow," Mom added.

"Never mind. I'll manage," I said.

At the dining room table, Mom filled my cup. "So how have you been? Are you settling in OK at Aunt Jean's?"

"I'm OK. Thanks for arranging it." I said.

Even as I made small talk, I felt fidgety. I was having a hard time breathing. I knew I wouldn't be able to stay long. As soon as I finished my tea, I stood up and said, "I have to go."

"Really? So soon? Are you sure?"

"I don't feel well. I'll come again."

They looked concerned. When the door closed behind me, I ran down the hall to the elevator. Outside, I gasped in deep breaths, as if I had been suffocating.

Aunt Jean and Uncle Sam lived in a row home only a few blocks away, and the walk helped me clear my mind. On the way, I stopped at the supermarket. I had expanded my diet from just fruit and nuts to include cottage cheese, which helped alleviate my incessant hunger.

With my shopping bag in hand, I tried slipping quietly behind my aunt and uncle. My aunt turned around to see me creeping up the stairs. "How was your visit?" she asked.

"Fine," I said, attempting to sound cheerful. I continued to my room, eager to get some food in my stomach and resume my meditation.

I clearly had not yet figured out how to live harmoniously with my family. For now, I had to keep meditating and reading. Hopefully after I was initiated, my life would fall into place.

Opening one of the books of questions and answers, I continued to study every iota of advice my spiritual teacher offered. In one passage, someone asked if it was OK to meditate before being initiated. Maharaj Ji suggested a temporary practice, which unfortunately, we were supposed to limit to fifteen minutes a day. I had tried my best to follow every single suggestion in every book, except I couldn't bring myself to obey this fifteen-minute restriction.

I clung to this temporary meditation, not only in order to return to God, but also to return to sanity. When I was repeating my mantra, I didn't feel consumed by worries, frustrations, and the general despair that had plagued me before I found the Path. I hoped Maharaj Ji would forgive me for disobeying this one rule.

I sat on the floor of my room for hours at a time and repeated the suggested mantra while focusing on the center of my forehead. When I could no longer hold my body erect, I slumped over and passed out. When I was able to rouse myself, I sat back up and repeated the cycle, alternating between sleep, meditation, and reading with an occasional visit to the bathroom. When I was hungry, I walked to the supermarket, brought back groceries, and ate in my room.

After a few weeks of this routine, my aunt knocked on my door to tell me an air letter had arrived from India. My heart raced as I tore open the flimsy blue paper. Maharaj Ji had accepted me. At last! It was going to happen. The journey of my soul would soon be fulfilled.

The letter instructed me to contact a representative to perform the ceremony. I scanned the list of representatives in the Path newsletter Jason had given me. The nearest one lived in Washington, D.C. His wife answered the phone and said she didn't know when he would be performing initiations. They would call me when he was ready. *But I'm ready now*, I thought impatiently.

I scanned the list again, hoping that I could find a representative to perform the ceremony right away. The next closest one was a thousand miles away in Minneapolis. Since I found the Path in Wisconsin, I thought it would be appropriate to be initiated in the Midwest.

Colonel Berg answered the phone. "I'm doing an initiation in a few days. But are you sure you want to fly all the way out here? There might be one closer to your home."

"I don't want to wait a day longer than I have to. I'll be there."

A few days later, I landed at the Minneapolis airport. A driver picked me up and we greeted each other with the gesture Jason had taught me, bringing palms together. During the ride, I silently repeated my temporary mantra. We entered an ordinary suburban middle-class home where several people waited for us. The atmosphere was relaxed and jovial.

Colonel Berg had a kind, even humble, manner that made me feel like we were equals. I wondered what had led him to the Path, and how he had qualified to become a representative of the guru. Despite my curiosity, I felt too preoccupied to engage in conversation. When the ceremony started, Colonel Berg explained that he was simply a vehicle, and that the true initiation was taking place between me and Maharaj Ji. He then proceeded to explain the vows not to eat meat, fish, or eggs, not to drink alcohol or take drugs except under a doctor's order, and not to engage in sex out of wedlock. Then he focused on the practice of meditation.

He said that my relationship with my teacher was sealed by the mantra. The mantra itself was the only secret information that I learned and he reminded me to never share it with anyone.

Another part of the meditation directed me to visualize my teacher. Just as repeating the mantra stills the verbal part of the mind, visualizing the teacher stills the visual part. But it wouldn't help to picture his photograph. Someday I would travel to India to meet him in person. Until then, I had to skip the visualization part of the meditation.

Even though I had read it all scattered throughout various books, I listened as carefully as if my life depended on it. Colonel Berg said that there was more going on than simply conveying information. By this commitment and this ceremony, my connection to my guru was established on higher planes. After years of floundering, I would now follow the Path, and my spiritual teacher would lead me beyond the wheel of reincarnation, and unite my soul with God.

I intended to treat the two-and-a-half-hour-a-day commitment to meditate as a minimum. I would extend that period as much as possible, and repeat the mantra every minute of the day. I knew it would be a long battle. The books predicted that my mind would dish up a steady flow of worries, plans, memories, and frustrations. Maharaj Ji said that stopping thoughts is futile, because they just build up with greater and greater pressure, like the water building up behind a dam. By meditating, I would relieve this pressure by diverting the thoughts toward God. This would take time.

Someday, instead of hearing only my own thoughts, I would hear God. The prospect of hearing God as an audible stream had appealed to me since that first night in Jason's apartment when I read the book about the Path. In the early stages, God might sound like wind blowing through the trees, or crickets through an open window, or the ringing sound a bell makes after it is struck. Eventually, the sound would evolve into celestial music, or an overpowering roar, like an airplane engine or a waterfall.

§§§

I appreciated the irony that I had been initiated into this spiritual path by a career officer in the U.S. military. A few years earlier, even knowing such a man would have been unthinkable. We would have stood on opposite ends of the universe, sworn enemies. But my ideas about all that had been changing, thanks to the fact that Maharaj Ji's own master had been a soldier in his younger years. So Colonel Berg's career didn't bother me. In fact, I looked at it with the same open mind as I approached all of the teachings of the Path, and saw more than just irony — I saw it as yet another example that on our journey to God, we are expected to accept our responsibility.

This rule to "do my duty" had already brought me back from the abyss of my own emotional chaos. Now that I was officially initiated, I knew I could no longer avoid Maharaj Ji's admonition to find my place in the world. I had to figure out how I was going to earn a living. I was afraid if I didn't push myself to leave my room, I was going to end up being a burden on my family, something the teachings of the Path specifically asked us to avoid.

A nearby department store hired me a few weeks before the Christmas season. All I had to do was walk to work and load boxes into people's cars. But I tired easily and took more breaks than other employees, during which I silently repeated the mantra. I hoped the job would be extended to a year-round position, so after Christmas I was disappointed that they couldn't keep me. I might need to behave more normally if I wanted to stay employed.

With no job, I continued to hole up in my aunt's guestroom, meditating, sleeping, and reading the books, hoping that Maharaj Ji's advice would help me figure out what to do next. He often recommended that we attend spiritual meetings, because the companionship of other initiates could help us stay focused.

I signed up for a free newsletter that listed meetings held in people's homes throughout the country. I called the number in the Philadelphia area. Vera, a woman with an elderly voice, encouraged me to attend the next meeting. The trip would involve several transfers on public transportation, but I didn't mind. I had nothing else to do, and wanted to be near other initiates.

There were only a few people there, and when it was time to start, Vera read from a book and gave a brief talk about the value of following the teachings. The other visitors, a young married couple and a man around my age, seemed preoccupied, and left immediately after the meeting. It felt good to be with people who shared my beliefs, but they all seemed as withdrawn as I was and offered little companionship.

I told Vera I was looking for work. She gave me the phone number of an initiate who told me about a foundry that might be hiring. "Don't worry about driving. It's near a train station."

"What's a foundry?" I asked.

"They pour molten metal into a cast. It's an ancient form of manufacturing."

"Interesting," I said, remembering my brief infatuation with molten metal during the ironworking class in Berkeley.

Receiving this suggestion from a fellow initiate felt like the next best thing to receiving it straight from Maharaj Ji. "I'll give it a try," I said, hoping it would involve less strenuous labor than carrying bars of steel on my shoulder.

When I told Aunt Jean that I was going to look for a job at a foundry, she gasped. "Oh no," she said and sat down, looking frightened.

"What's wrong?"

"When I was a little girl in Russia, so many men were injured or killed in those places. When one of the men got a job in the local foundry, all the women would huddle together and cry."

"Oh, Jean," I said, wanting to reassure her. "That's terrible. It's not that way here."

Her comment didn't scare me about myself—this was America, and I didn't expect foundries to be dangerous. But her frightened memory gave me a sobering reminder of the miserable conditions my grandparents fled, and gratitude that we had landed in a country where workers were protected.

I took a train to a town north of the city and walked a couple of miles to the workshop. It wasn't much bigger than an automobile service station, with dirt floors, rough wooden walls, and only a couple of employees. The owner showed me how they pressed sand into molds. The furnaces were shut down so I didn't see them actually pouring the metal.

On my way out, he said he'd think about hiring me. The next day when I called, he told me he changed his mind and decided he didn't need anyone. I thought about my lean body and I supposed he could tell I had vision problems.

My job opportunities were too limited as long as I was living on the outskirts of the city. Perhaps if I moved to the center of the city, it would be easier to find work. I gathered my clothes along with my books about the Path into a backpack, and saying goodbye, I went into Philadelphia to look for a place to live.

How to Earn a Living

In a phone booth, I flipped open the Yellow Pages to "yoga center," hoping to find a place where I could meditate with spiritually oriented people. I called and begged the man who answered to put me up for the night. The man said "I'm sorry, but no. We're not set up for that." I pleaded, throwing in a reference to my need for a quiet place to meditate. He gave in. The place was in West Philadelphia near the University of Pennsylvania.

It was in a three-story row home from an older era, with wooden banisters and porches. This part of the city always smelled funny, as though the rain and the old paint and a hundred years of habitation had permeated the streets.

A bearded man opened the door of the commune, and looked me over. I imagined he might be having second thoughts about inviting me to stay. But my gratitude and desperation gave him an extra push, and without smiling, he showed me to a room on the third floor. I closed the door and sat to meditate. The house grew quiet. Finally when I could meditate no more, I passed out. Hours later, I was awakened by people talking, doors closing, chairs moving. I looked at the clock. It was three a.m., time for me to get up and start meditating.

After I went to the bathroom, I sat on the floor. Downstairs, they began to chant. Of all the places in the city, I had picked a spiritual community whose morning schedule disrupted mine. I soldiered on through my own meditation, doing my best to stay centered. At dawn, I gathered my things, dropped a few dollars in the donation box, and left.

All morning, I walked around the University campus, a part of the city that had given me some of the best memories in my high school years. I scanned bulletin boards for an apartment and went to see one a few blocks from campus. It had a kitchen table, a couple of chairs, and a mattress on the floor. I rented it right away.

The next day, I walked the twenty blocks to Center City, looking at every storefront. The pleasant walk led through a quaint part of town near the well-maintained park at Rittenhouse Square. I had no chance of being hired at places where they sold swanky houseware or clothing. But when I passed a gift store that had an artistic look, I thought it was worth a try.

My hopes increased when I met the manager, who had a shaggy beard, cheerful smile, and twinkling eyes. I told him about my work experience on the loading dock of the department store. He chuckled when I mentioned my bachelor's degree in physics. It was a jovial, kind-hearted laugh, as if he was in on a joke. I told him I wasn't wearing glasses because I wanted to improve my vision. He gave me a job stocking shelves and packing gifts for shipping. He didn't seem to mind that I had to squint and lean in close to read labels.

Anytime I wasn't working, I stayed in the apartment and slept, meditated, or read books about the Path. The books were filled with devotional insights from people like Rumi, Kabir, Hafiz, and Shams-i Tabrizi. In addition to feeling inspired by them, I was learning how mystics throughout the ages have consistently said that the real bliss of the human experience is not out here in worldly success or comfort, but inside in our connection with God.

One night, I came home to find a letter that had been forwarded from my parents' address. It was from Pepper, the sister of the woman with whom I had been in love in California. From the first time I met Pepper, I felt like we had been old friends, but after my disastrous breakup, what could she possibly have to write about? I opened the letter and read about how she knew I had always been desperate to find some true north. She said she found a spiritual path that might interest me. When she told me the name of her teacher, I felt the mysteries of the universe collide, in one of those coincidences that only make sense when you take into account the hand of an unseen guide. How could I have fallen in love with Patricia in California, and then found an obscure Eastern teaching in Madison, and then a year later, after having moved to Philadelphia, Patricia's sister writes to tell me about the same group? I wrote back and told her we were already on the same wavelength.

Over the next couple of months, I relaxed my dietary restrictions, slipping bread and cooked vegetables into the mix. It felt good to be eating more substantial food. My constant hunger began to subside and I felt stronger. Gradually, the fatigue that had plagued me in Berkeley began to lift, and I was able to walk around town with as much energy as I had before my collapse.

I had to face the fact that my eyes were not improving. I was sure that in such a large city, I would find someone to coach me on Aldous Huxley's system of eye exercises. After scouring the phone book, though, I was only able to find one ad for an optometrist who might be able to help. After hours of bus transfers to his office in the Northeast section of the city, I explained my situation. He said he had never heard proof that Huxley's method actually worked. When even he recommended glasses, I relented. I put on the glasses he prescribed for me and the world suddenly burst into focus. I could see street signs so I knew where I was. I could see the expression on people's faces, making it easier to relate to them. And it was a thousand times easier to read. It was like a miracle.

Wearing glasses brought another change. As soon as I was able to see more clearly, my mind felt sharper too, as if I were awakening from a long sleep. I no longer felt satisfied packing boxes. I wanted to challenge myself mentally. Just because I wasn't going to be a doctor didn't mean I needed to stop thinking.

From the help wanted ads in the newspaper, I found an employment agency that promised entry-level computer jobs. I sat in a large room with a crowd of applicants, and when it was my turn, I went to talk to a young man in a suit and tie.

"Your shirt is wrinkled," he said. "And the way you squint makes me feel like you're looking through me." I smiled politely, unsure if he was insulting me or coaching me. He continued, "I know of a company that would hire you to work in a chemical processing plant."

His suggestion made me shudder. I couldn't imagine myself surrounded by the harsh smells. I walked out, disappointed by his lack of regard for my feelings or job interests. I vowed to steer clear of job agencies.

One ad that looked promising came from a small publishing company. When I went to the interview on Washington Square in Philadelphia, I was delighted by the nearby tiny park. Somehow I had missed this gem of urban beauty tucked away in the historic heart of the city.

The manager who had placed the ad asked me about my experience and I told him I worked at the college newspaper. He gave me a tour of the small office, and said, "You know, Curtis Publishing is just down the street. Years ago, this section of Philadelphia was an important publishing hub of the United States."

"No, I didn't know that," I said, feeling a stirring of pride.

"We publish catalogs for various organizations. Your job will be to proofread the entries to ensure their accuracy." It sounded more intellectually stimulating than working in a gift shop so I accepted.

In one of my first projects, I edited the membership catalog for the American College of Cardiology, looking for typos. I wondered if my older brother belonged to the organization. Sure enough, I proofread the spelling of his name, Edward B. Waxler. I loved coincidences, although this one came with a bittersweet irony. Despite my passion for science and my degree in physics, I was getting paid pennies a name to review the spelling of my cardiologist-brother's listing.

After a few weeks I asked my boss if I could work on something more challenging. "Nope. This is it."

Every day at lunch, I went for long walks. Instead of wondering about the history of each building, as I had done in high school, now I wondered if a business inside might play a role in my future. I didn't know exactly what I was looking for and hoped the right situation would present itself.

One sunny day I walked past an office building on Broad Street a block north of City Hall. Next to the doorway a small brass plaque said, "United Engineers and Constructors." I had heard of this company — Larry's father worked there. In high school, Larry encouraged me to go to the University of Wisconsin, one of the most important decisions of my life. Now, here I was standing in front of United Engineers, where his father worked. Wouldn't it be strange if I followed Larry here, too?

One reason I loved physics was because of its fabulous explanations for physical phenomena, such as electricity and heat. But physics offered boring explanations for coincidences, attributing them to the rules of haphazard chance. The laws of karma and reincarnation offered much more interesting explanations. Now, I saw coincidences as expressions of our connections with each other. We were all crossing paths, paying off debts, continuing in one life where we left off in a past one. Based on these principles, I speculated that Larry and I must have had many past life connections.

But just because something in past lives set this destiny in motion, didn't mean I knew how it would turn out. I entered the building and asked the receptionist for an application. When I came to the question about who recommended me, I named Larry's father. It felt good. I had a degree, a connection with a senior member of the firm, and I wasn't asking for much money. United Engineers was expanding rapidly to fulfill orders for the booming nuclear power business. They hired me immediately. A real job! I was on my way to figuring out my life. "Thank you Larry," I shouted to him across the eons. "My karma with you must be very strong."

I started as a clerk in the computer analysis department, which mainly consisted of sitting at my desk until the phone rang. The secretary answered the phone, wrote down some information, and handed me the slip of paper. I rode the elevator to the engineering floor and picked up a stack of computer cards from one of the guys in cubicles.

All the engineers took a moment to thank me and ask me how I was doing. I felt good around these guys, several of whom seemed to be reaching out to me with an almost fatherly protectiveness.

I rode the elevator to the floor with the computers and entered the refrigerator-cold room, flooded with noise from fans and card readers. I filled out a form and handed it, along with the cards, to the guy behind the counter. "How long do you think it will be?" I shouted to be heard above the din.

He grimaced but didn't respond. I asked again, louder. "Excuse me. How long will it be?"

"About twenty minutes," he finally said without looking up.

I watched him place the deck into a tray and slip a pressure plate against them. With a swoosh and clatter, the stack of cards were sucked into the machine, reappearing seconds later in the output tray. The operator ran back and forth between these card bins and the printer behind him, which banged away with a machine-gun staccato, spewing paper into the tray in front. The operator riffled through the printouts, tearing off each job with a satisfying rip. Then he bundled the printer paper and computer deck, snapped a rubber band around the pack, and piled it on the stack. I grabbed it, rode the elevator to the engineering floor, and handed it to the engineer, who smiled again and thanked me. Then I went back to my desk to wait for another request.

One day, when I went to the cubicles to deliver a printout, the engineer gave me a friendly smile and asked me how I was doing. When Chet spoke, I noticed a strong accent but at first I couldn't place why it sounded different. I had been away in Wisconsin for four years, and California for two, and now that I was settling back in, I realized that Philadelphians have an accent. I started to laugh, but caught myself, not wanting to look strange. Since he was being so friendly, I asked him if he had a minute.

"Sure," he said.

"What do you do, exactly?"

"Pull up a chair. I'll show you."

Pointing to the engineering drawing rolled out on his desk, he said, "These drawings represent the pipes in a power plant. These symbols," he said, pointing along the pipeline, "represent valves. And these here are couplings."

"What's a coupling?"

He pulled a book from his desk drawer. "You can see pictures of all this stuff in this catalog." He flipped through it to show me. "I use this book all the time. The most important hardware for us are the hangers," he said, flipping to a different section of the book. "Our job is to make sure they don't break."

"How do you figure it out?"

"We run all the piping information through a computer and the computer checks to make sure their placement is safe. If it finds a problem, we make some adjustments and run it again."

"What sort of problem?"

He looked through his printout. "Here's a simple example: The pipe is too heavy for the hangers. That's easy to fix. Just add more hangers. A more complicated problem happens when a hot pipe expands. We have to specify hangers that allow it to slide."

Ah. My years in physics were paying off. I could easily understand the forces on these pipes.

"The most important thing is to make sure the hangers don't break during an earthquake."

"Are you serious? How can the computer know that?"

173

Chet shrugged. "I'm no expert. I've heard that the computer runs the pipe through a sample earthquake and calculates the forces."

I went back to my desk excited by the curiosity swirling through my mind. Chet's job looked far more interesting than mine. Since I had to work anyway, perhaps I could get a job that would teach me new things, and enable me to work with people who were kind?

The next time I made a delivery to Chet, a drawing of a pipe run was spread out on his desk.

I lingered again, and his relaxed manner made it easy to ask him more questions. "The one thing I still haven't figured out is how you create the computer decks," I said.

He stood up and leaned over the large drawing. "All those little red circles are my handiwork," he said with a big smile. "Here, I'll show you." In one hand he held a small green plastic sheet with various sizes of circles cut out. In the other, he held a red pencil. He placed the green plastic template on the drawing, drew the circle, and stood back to survey it. Gesturing dramatically he said, "Voila."

"I draw a circle at each hanger, and number it. That information is punched onto the computer cards that you take to the computer room."

"What do you do with the thick printouts that I bring back? You can't possibly read all those numbers."

He flipped to the back page and pointed to the word "Warning" in capital letters surrounded by asterisks. He lowered his voice. "This is the only page I look at. The rest of the report is just wasted paper."

I lowered my voice, not sure if I could get in trouble for asking. "Do you think I could get a job doing this?"

"Sure. They're hiring. Why don't you go ask Ollie?"

For the next few days, hardly any requests for computer decks came in and I had a lot of time to sit at my desk and think. I wondered if my degree in physics would be sufficient to qualify for the job. And I worried about departmental politics. Would the company allow me to switch to a different position? But trading in this boring job for an interesting one seemed like an obvious choice.

Finally, I got up my courage and went to Ollie's office. Ollie, like the others, was always kind to me. He was bald, with a round face, soft eyes and a gentle smile. "Yes, Jerry?" He recognized me from my frequent visits to the department.

"I wonder if there is any chance I could get a job here."

He invited me to sit down, and we talked for a few minutes about my qualifications. He said my degree in physics was excellent and he would be delighted to have me.

After a visit to the personnel office, I moved into the row of cubicles. I was delighted that Chet would be my cubicle mate. From him, I learned how to do pipe stress analysis. I also learned what it meant to be a working man.

"When I saw you coming around picking up computer cards," he told me, "it reminded me of the way I started. United Engineers hired me right after high school. My first job was to wheel around a cart, delivering prints to the designers."

"So how did you go from carting drawings to becoming an engineer?"

"After a few months of hanging around and watching the guys drawing blueprints, one of them gave me a chance to draw a few lines. Gradually they gave me more difficult assignments. I got married and had kids. And at the same time, I went to night school, paid for by United Engineers. It took eight years to get my degree and a few more to become a professional engineer."

I compared his life to mine. When I left college, I embraced the hippie philosophy that money doesn't matter and work is everyone else's problem. Thanks to Maharaj Ji's advice, I was finally trying to do my duty to family and society. Chet knew all about that responsibility and I hoped some of his work ethic would rub off on me.

One day, after I had successfully completed a few pipe stress tests, Chet looked at me with a grin and said, "There's an old expression, 'Six months ago, I couldn't spell enginar. Now I are one.'"

He was smiling but I didn't get the joke.

He repeated himself, mispronouncing each syllable with comical exaggeration: "en . . . guy . . . nar . . ." I realized it was true. Last year, I had no idea what I wanted to do, and now I was working as a pipe stress analyst. The humor of the situation struck me so hard, I burst into laughter. Not wanting to disturb my fellow workers, I ran to the bathroom, where my body shook with waves of laughter. After all these years of uncertainty, of struggle, of not being sure I even wanted a job, I was finally able to call myself something. I was an engineer.

Where Is My Group

After work, I fixed a meal of vegetables and rice, and went to bed early so I could wake up before dawn and meditate. Most Saturdays, I was too restless to spend the whole day meditating, so I took the subway into Center City, and went for long walks. Sundays I went to meetings with other followers of the Path.

The group run by Vera was pleasant, but so stodgy I didn't feel I could relate to anyone there. I phoned the guy who told me about the job at the foundry and asked him if he knew of younger initiates. He told me there was a commune near the University of Pennsylvania and he thought they might be willing to talk to me. I met him on campus and together we walked over to an old row home at 3721 Chestnut Street, next door to a red brick church. The apartment's dark blue ceiling was decorated with stars, and mattresses on the floors served as sofas. It reminded me of the student apartments in Madison.

A grinding screech emerged from the back of the house. We went through the kitchen into a small utility room where a tall, thin man wearing goggles was leaning over a grindstone. Sparks were flying from the object he held in his hands. My friend shouted. "David, this is Jerry." The man at the grindstone looked up and gave me a big, toothy grin. Then he looked down and kept working. Like other initiates I had met, he seemed too busy to talk.

When we walked out of the room, my friend said, "He's grinding buckles. That foundry I told you about is one of our suppliers."

That explained how he knew the owner of the foundry, but it didn't help me get any companionship. "Could I hang out with any of the people who live here?"

"They pretty much keep to themselves," he said. "None of them go to meetings anymore."

Disappointed by this dead end, the following weekend, I took the train to New York City. There were about 60 initiates and seekers at the meeting there, the most I had ever seen in one room. Many of them were young, and looked like they ought to be interesting. When the meeting adjourned, I joined a few of them at a restaurant for lunch. They seemed to know each other, or at least knew what to say to each other. I felt too awkward to speak and silently repeated my mantra.

Without finding any relief for my loneliness in New York, I called the phone number listed for the Washington, D.C. group. The guy who answered seemed friendly enough. "Sure. Come on down. A number of us live together in group homes. You're welcome to spend the night here on Saturday night and go with us to *satsang* Sunday." Despite the longer distance, I decided to give it a try.

When they welcomed me into their living room, I immediately felt more at home than I had in other groups. The next day, Sunday, it got even better. For *satsang*, we went to a home with a large living room where about 40 people around my age had gathered. They seemed to be having fun.

There were a number of communal houses nearby, some with women and others with men. The guy who had invited me said that if I was interested in moving here, I might be able to find an opening. But I already had a job in Philadelphia. And my purpose for moving east was to be in the same city with my parents. So far I didn't have much success connecting with them, but I wanted to keep trying. I decided moving to Washington would be too disruptive.

Another Sunday, I took the bus to a small meeting in central New Jersey. The guy who picked me up from the bus station seemed friendly, and the people at the meeting seemed like a lively bunch.

During the meeting, someone read a passage from Plato, about people chained inside a cave in such a way that the only thing they could see were the shadows cast against the wall. One of those people escaped. At first it was too bright to see, but gradually he acclimated to the sun and realized that the things he had been seeing his whole life were mere shadows. Filled with wonder, he went back inside the cave, excited to share what he had seen. However, the people who were chained inside mocked him for his foolish beliefs.

As Plato put it, "Were he to return there, wouldn't he be rather bad at their game, no longer being accustomed to the darkness? Wouldn't it be said of him that he went up and came back with his eyes corrupted, and that it's not even worth trying to go up?"

We all laughed at the story, delighted that Socrates had so eloquently described our own lives. Like the man who had escaped the cave, we too had realized our lives were shadows of the real thing. But when we tried to go back into the world and live normally, we felt out of place.

One of the initiates said, "It's a hassle finding vegetarian food, trying to make time to meditate, and tiptoeing around our belief system when we visit our parents." We all nodded.

This is why I came to these meetings, to be around other people who were looking for the same insights that I was. And at the meeting, I had learned something new: Plato was teaching the Path. Until now, I had mainly heard about teachers who lived in the Middle East or in India. Now I was delighted to discover that the mystical path was also known in ancient Greece. I loved the way the Path tied together wisdom from so many different places and times.

After the meeting, we drank tea together, but I was my usual clumsy self, unable to contribute to the conversation. By the end I had not made any friends. This excursion, like all my other attempts to find a group, helped me feel connected to the Path, but when I went home, I was just as alone as ever. Even though I had moved to the city where I grew up, I still had not found my home.

§§§

One month, when the monthly Path newsletter arrived, I saw a new listing for a meeting an hour's ride by train from Philadelphia. I called the number and a man with a heavy Indian accent picked up. I told him I wanted to attend his meeting and he said, "Oh, yes, please join us. I'll pick you up from the train station."

That Sunday, as promised, Sanjay was waiting for me. He had nut-brown skin, a round, pocked face, and kind eyes. He quickly pressed his palms together, and bowed his head. I did the same, a shared gesture that instantly set me at ease.

"I'm so glad you could come," he said. "We just moved to the area and I want as many people as possible to come to my house for meetings." He spoke fast and emphatically, as if every sentence was important. His enthusiastic, welcoming words lifted me out of my isolation.

We climbed the stairs to his apartment. His wife was there, wearing a traditional Indian sari. I had seen many pictures of life in India and I was familiar with the long flowing garment of colorful fabric, but this was the first time I greeted someone wearing one. She smiled warmly and offered me the traditional greeting, clasping her hands together and bowing slightly. She tittered but did not speak.

Hovering around her were three children, a little girl wearing glasses, a little boy, and a toddler. Another couple was sitting on the sofa. They both smiled and returned my greeting. The amazing thing was that they asked me about myself and they seemed interested in my answer. This was a new experience. There was a knock on the door. Sanjay ran to answer it, greeting the newcomers with such energy they all broke into laughter.

About ten of us assembled for the meeting. Most sat on the sofa or chairs, while Sanjay and I sat cross-legged on the floor, a posture that helped me concentrate. He opened by asking us to pause for a few moments of silent meditation. This was my favorite part, sitting with others trying to reach inside for the presence of God. Then he read from one of the books about the power of God's love, and how our souls are drops in the ocean of love. After the reading, Sanjay talked about his love for Maharaj Ji. One young woman said, "I am so grateful to be here. I don't know where I would be if I had not found this Path." Everyone nodded.

"The key is to meditate," Sanjay said. "As our master always says, by repeating the mantra during meditation and throughout the day, you will find all the answers inside." After the meeting, Sanjay invited us to stay for lunch. I eagerly accepted the invitation, delighted to feel part of this family. They laid newspaper on the carpet and we sat cross-legged on the floor. The generous servings of rice, *dal*, and *pekoras* were savory and filling.

Sanjay didn't seem to mind my quiet spells or my interest in only talking about the spiritual teachings. In fact, he seemed more focused on the topic than I was. His joy made me realize that I didn't need to be so serious. It was possible to focus on the Path and still be happy. His charm lifted me, and in his home I could relax and just be myself.

I left the meeting feeling a wave of relief, as if my search had ended. Just a short train ride away, I could join other people who shared my beliefs and who welcomed me into their midst. I counted the days until the next meeting. When it arrived, and Sanjay again picked me up from the station, and each meeting, I felt closer to him, his family, and the group he was gathering. Between meetings, I now had something to look forward to. The anticipation helped me stay out of the dark pit of depression from which I had recently emerged.

§§§

One Sunday morning, when Sanjay picked me up, he seemed more excited than usual. Smiling so wide I didn't think he could squeeze another morsel of joy into his face, he said, "I have some incredible news. You know Katherine Windress, the author of *The Living Master?*"

"Yes, of course. It was her book that turned me on to the Path." I remembered the miracle of that night in Madison when Jason told me he had a new master.

"She lives near here. I have been calling her for weeks, pleading with her to come to the meeting. She said she had not attended any public gathering for several years." His voice took on a joyful tone, like a small child talking about receiving a wonderful gift. "She said that thanks to my insistence, she will come."

I tried to grasp the enormity of what Sanjay was saying. Katherine Windress? I was going to meet Katherine Windress? In person? It seemed too good to be true. Most of the initiates I had met had never even seen Maharaj Ji. Katherine not only met him, but spent years with him in India. In her book, she reported extensive conversations between Maharaj Ji and the Westerners. Now, by meeting her, I would be only one step away from being in his presence.

I didn't know what to say, so I sat quietly trying to say my mantra, but my thoughts kept interrupting with the joy and mysteries of this Path. How did I end up here in the same place as the author of the book that saved me? Another karmic thread, picking up from some past life. And another reason to feel grateful to God for guiding me back from the abyss, and then providing me with this connection that would help me grow.

Soon after we returned to Sanjay's apartment, Katherine and her husband David arrived. Both of them were tall and thin, with blazing smiles. I was surprised to see they were about my age. I was expecting someone much older. Katherine had straight blond hair and beautiful blue eyes. The most remarkable thing about her was her enthusiasm. She seemed as excited to meet everyone, as we were to meet her.

"Please call me Kathy," she said. The familiar form of her name made her seem even more accessible. Despite the fact that she was an attractive woman, I didn't feel intimidated by her.

Instead she exuded some sort of joy and depth that made me feel like I was in the presence of an old friend.

David was handsome, with wavy, brown hair, a square jaw, and a big dimple in the middle of his chin. This was the same man I met in Philadelphia, grinding buckles in the back room of an apartment. He seemed alert and yet relaxed. His smile was just as warm as Kathy's, but there was also something mischievous about him, as if he were looking to turn every moment into a joke.

Around Kathy and David, Sanjay's attitude of service and devotion increased a hundredfold. He kept thanking them for coming and repeatedly told them what an honor it was to have them in his home. He was so exuberant, I wouldn't have been surprised to see him open the window and shout with joy.

Sanjay attempted to restore his composure and after a few minutes, he calmed down and gave Kathy and David a chance to take off their coats and settle down. Sanjay's wife smiled shyly. To my surprise, Kathy spoke a few words to her in Hindi, and Sanjay's wife burst into laughter.

Kathy and David attempted to keep up with all the introductions. Finally, we settled down, and when everyone was seated, Sanjay asked Kathy to tell us about her time with Maharaj Ji. She tried to demur, saying she was just one of us and was glad to participate in such a loving group. Sanjay insisted on turning the meeting over to her, begging her to share whatever she could.

She told us that when she lived in India, she'd spent time with Maharaj Ji at his spiritual village as well as on some of his tours around India. She also toured with him on his trip to the United States. She said those experiences were the most precious times in her life, but the most important thing was that we had all been blessed with the grace of having been initiated. When she talked about our shared blessing of being under his guidance, she used the same breathless phrasing that made her book so inspiring. "He is with us right now," she said, and we all grew quiet, feeling a wave of peace.

But Sanjay broke the silence. "Please, please, could you tell us just one story?" His childlike plea, backed up by our echoes of agreement, broke through Kathy's attempt to remain out of the limelight.

She said, "OK, here's, one." We giggled in anticipation. "Once when Maharaj Ji was in Atlantic City, we were riding in a car and I said, 'Look Maharaj Ji, there's a church on the right, and a bar on the left.' I thought I was being so clever, and assumed he would say something about how the right is always better. But instead he laughed and said, 'Let's go straight ahead and jump in the ocean.'" When Kathy told us his punch line, we all burst into laughter.

That story opened my eyes to Maharaj Ji's lightness and joy, along with his brilliance. Instead of dwelling on ethics or even on worship, his metaphor gently brought Kathy's attention back to the central goal of the Path, to merge in the ocean of God's love. The story also opened me to a new vision of my relationship to the Path. Or rather it reminded me of that vision.

The very first thing I ever read about the Path was the description of Kathy sitting with a dozen disciples in his rose garden asking him questions. Since then, I had read many books by Maharaj Ji about the journey of the soul, and the importance of meditation. And I had attended many meetings in which disciples spoke of embracing these principles, but today's meeting was the first time I had met someone who had been with Maharaj Ji in a private setting. Now, instead of imagining him at a distance, surrounded by hundreds of thousands of disciples,

Kathy brought him to life as a person. I felt a longing to meet him someday, and if I couldn't be around him, at least I could be around her.

At the end of the meeting, Sanjay said to Kathy and David, "You'll come back, of course." The room grew quiet, hoping for her agreement. When she said, "I'd love to," all of us erupted in cheers. I had definitely found my home.

People at the House

Each meeting at Sanjay's house felt so full of energy, so charming and intense. Usually after the regular program of reading from one of the books, we begged Kathy for more stories. These turned out to be less plentiful than I had hoped. She always tried to deflect the conversation from her personal stories and instead emphasized the importance of devotion to Maharaj Ji and the Path.

"He is available to everyone by going inside during meditation," she said, trying to distract us from pestering her. Her encouragement to look inside ourselves didn't deter us from begging for more glimpses of Maharaj Ji. If she talked about devotion, someone would say, "Then tell us a story about devotion," and as usual, everyone laughed.

She occasionally gave in. "OK. One time, I went with Maharaj Ji to see a concert by the famous sitar player, Ravi Shankar. We were sitting in the front row. During an intermission, when Maharaj Ji excused himself, I was sitting there alone. Ravi Shankar was still on the stage and he gestured to me. At first, I couldn't understand what he wanted. He was pointing to Maharaj Ji's shawl. I touched it and raised my eyebrows and he nodded. So I picked it up. He came to the edge of the stage, and took it from me, and held it close to his face for a moment. Then with a big smile he handed it to me, and I put it back on Maharaj Ji's chair."

We sat hushed, trying to imagine this legendary musician having such respect for our teacher. Kathy was quiet for a few moments and said, "That's the whole point. It's all about devotion."

Occasionally she brought in photos of her with Maharaj Ji, an intriguing glimpse into a past, little more than ten years earlier when there were only a dozen Westerners at the ashram at any one time. The real prize was a silent home movie she showed us of the time she had accompanied him on his 1964 tour of the United States. One clip showed Maharaj Ji, Kathy, and one of Maharaj Ji's representatives walking on the boardwalk in Atlantic City. They were laughing at the camera, almost clowning around. In another scene Maharaj Ji was sitting with small American children on a sofa in someone's living room. The children, instead of being put off by his turban and long beard, seemed attracted to him. He was laughing and patting them on the head, looking almost childlike himself. I wondered if they could feel his spirituality. Perhaps they had residual vision from previous lives, which had not yet been clouded in their new births.

I had seen many photos of Maharaj Ji and one or two movies of him delivering spiritual discourses to an audience, but this was the first informal video I had ever seen. In it, he was more lighthearted than I imagined.

After the meeting one Sunday, Kathy and David invited everyone to come up to their house. Several of us agreed. David said he would be glad to drop me off at the train station so I could get back to my apartment in Philadelphia. On the drive to their place we passed miles of farmland and woods. When we drove up their long dirt driveway, I was enchanted by the trees surrounding us.

Upstairs in the living room, the cathedral ceiling and the big picture windows made it feel like we were up in the trees. Kathy sat at the baby grand piano and played gorgeous classical pieces by Chopin, Liszt, and Beethoven. I listened, mesmerized by the intensity with which she threw herself into the keyboard. When she stopped we applauded and told her how beautifully she played. She told us that until recently she had been a piano teacher at the Settlement Music School in Philadelphia.

After Kathy's impromptu recital, she excused herself. She had to go to her office and write. The others said goodbye and then David disappeared. I had an hour to kill before I had to catch the train so I went outside, and down trails through the woods behind the house. I felt comforted by the presence of trees, and gentle touch of leaves. When it was time to go, I found David reading in his room. He jumped up to drive me. On the way out, I saw Kathy in her office surrounded by books, typing at a big electric typewriter. She looked up and smiled and said, "Come again soon."

§§§

After every meeting at Sanjay's house, David and Kathy extended an open invitation to anyone who wanted to visit. I always accepted. In the living room, Kathy always played the piano. Afterward, if she lingered, I asked her questions about the Path. Since she was always trying to get back to her writing, I asked her about that, too.

"The last time I was with Maharaj Ji," she said, "he asked me to write another book for him. He said this one should be about Jesus. I decided to write from the point of view of the disciples."

"How can you develop a whole story about their lives?" I asked, trying to imagine how anyone could build characters from just the few glimpses that were offered in the Bible.

"Come on, I'll show you," she said, and we went into the spare bedroom that had been converted into her office. She gestured to the stacks of books balanced on every surface in her office.

"Based on these books about his life and times plus a close reading of the Bible, I created this map," she said pointing to a hand-drawn poster on her wall. "This tracks Jesus' journey through ancient Judea."

"But how can you balance history with your imagination?"

"The disciples were like us, trying to follow the teachings of a master. I imagine what we might feel like around Maharaj Ji and develop scenes based on my understanding of a mystical relationship between teacher and student."

During these regular visits to the house, I also got to know David. He was an expert at teasing, and whenever he walked into a room, his verbal sparring and joking turned every conversation into a pleasant buzz. I was always so stiff around people, I hoped some of his bantering might rub off on me.

By the end of the afternoon, when it was time for me to catch my train, Kathy was back at her typewriter. When I said goodbye to her, sometimes she gave me a big smile, but just as often, she was so engaged in her writing that she barely looked up. As soon as David dropped me off at the train, I started missing the house.

After a few months, they invited a young woman who was attending Sanjay's meetings to move into the guest room. Soon they invited a couple to move into the den and Kathy moved her desk and books out to the garage, which she set up like an office.

Every time I visited, something else was going on. People were moving into apartments nearby and within a year of our first meeting, the place was turning into a community.

§§§

I grew fond of these Sunday afternoon visits to the house, hoping that Kathy would linger in the living room so I could ask her questions. Occasionally I found myself alone with her, which were especially precious times for me. On one such occasion, she told me about living in Boston. It turned out she was a few years older than I was, and in 1960, she was twenty years old. She spent hours in bookstores, looking for insights into consciousness. During one of those forays, she found a book about the Path and after reading it, she became crazy to know more.

At the time, she was in love with a Greek man who was bewildered by her inquiry into otherworldly topics. His name was Elias. My mind went into full alert. That was the name of the Greek guy who lived downstairs from me in Madison, and who was with me when I was beaten up. Then she mentioned his last name, and I almost passed out. No two people could have that name. I closed my eyes, trying to make sense of what had just happened.

How could this be possible? I asked Kathy more about him. She said he was a physics major at Harvard. It was definitely the same guy, and yet it couldn't be. Finally, I broke in, so excited I could barely speak.

"I knew Elias, too."

She looked surprised. "You knew Elias?"

"Yes, yes, yes. In Madison."

Kathy smiled. "Tell me about him," she said.

"When I knew him, he had switched his field of study. He was a mathematician. He helped me with my math homework. A really nice, gentle man."

"How did he look?"

My brain was exploding trying to grasp all of this.

"He looked good. His hair was thinning a little. But help me understand: You knew Elias thirteen years ago in Boston, and I knew him six years ago in Madison, Wisconsin. That's crazy."

She didn't seem confused. "That's karma, Jer. Links that seem coincidental all have some past reason."

Calmed by the way she was accepting the outlandish coincidence, I thought about it more, remembering back to the time I talked to Elias and asked him for help with a math problem. Then I remembered standing on the porch outside the apartment, and accepting his offer to go for a walk. Suddenly, I realized there was another layer to the coincidence.

"Oh my God. It keeps getting stranger. That apartment where I was living upstairs from Elias in 1967," I sputtered, trying to untangle all the connections. "Jason was my roommate. Jason is the guy who would later give me your book about Maharaj Ji. That's what turned me onto the Path."

"Why are you so surprised, Jerry? You know that feeling when you meet someone for the first time and are sure you've known them before? That's because you actually have. We come to this world to work off the karma that we created in past lives, and that means we often interact with people we have known for many lifetimes."

"But this situation is so extreme," I said. This moment felt stranger than anything I had experienced while I was taking drugs. It reminded me of a passage in a book I read when I was stoned during my college years. In *Steppenwolf* by Hermann Hesse, the character saw a mysterious doorway with a sign on it that read, "Price of admission: your mind" and he walked in. That's how I felt today.

I loved the cosmic connections that Maharaj Ji kept sending my way. Perhaps it was his way of keeping in touch.

I wanted to spend more time near the community Kathy and David had created. I found an apartment halfway between my job in the city and their house in the country. David loaned me his van to move my few belongings.

Every weekday, I walked down to the train station and commuted to Philadelphia. I didn't mind the long ride. I read a book or meditated. On weekends David and Kathy picked me up and drove me to spiritual meetings. Eventually, David helped me find a used car. Now, in addition to driving myself to Sanjay's for meetings, I was able to drive to David and Kathy's house.

I Moved In

In the summer of 1974, Kathy and David received permission to visit the Maharaj Ji's spiritual community in the northwest of India. That September, a number of us stood in the driveway, hugged them, and waved goodbye. Kathy was bringing her manuscript. During their three-month visit, she intended to ask Maharaj Ji for feedback to help write the book.

While they were in India, I submitted my own request for permission to visit the village. Each day, I took the train home from United Engineers, and on the way into my apartment, I checked the mail. In November, as I approached the mailbox, I had a weird sensation as if I were watching a movie and someone had jiggered a few frames. When I pulled my hand out of the box, I held the powder-blue letter as delicately as if it were a missive from God. I opened it slowly. It contained the invitation I had been waiting for. In January, I would meet my master.

My boss agreed to give me a leave of absence. I dug out my passport and bought a plane ticket. I also had to decide what to do about my apartment. Leaving it vacant for three months seemed like a waste of money, so I decided to move to Kathy and David's house. A half dozen people were already living there and I didn't think David would mind one more, especially considering I would leave for India about the same time they returned. I moved in to a spare room, and continued to commute to work through December.

I had ignored many roommates over the years. Now, I wanted to be accepted by these fellow travelers on the Path, but was not having much success figuring out how to become friends with any of them.

There was one attractive woman on whom I became fixated. Even though we had only exchanged pleasantries and never had a real conversation, I decided that I would like to marry her. After a month at the house, I asked her if she would go for a walk. Out in the woods, I proposed. Her eyes widened and she drew back. "Oh, Jerry," she said, pausing. Finally she said, "Absolutely not." I felt humiliated and realized I had blundered. I had no idea how to connect with women. Loneliness felt like a permanent feature of my life.

One night, late in December, I was awakened by a commotion. I went to the living room to investigate. Pulling open the sliding glass door, I saw it was snowing lightly, and Kathy and David were coming up the stairs. They both looked tired after the long flight from India, but they brightened when they saw me. I was happy to see them but I was in an awkward position. David didn't know I was living there. Nervously I explained that I had given up my apartment in anticipation of going to India, and was living at the house. He went along with it without hesitation, graciously accepting his surprise houseguest.

The next day, David went off to resume his duties at his buckle company. I had already stopped working in anticipation of my imminent trip to India. That enabled me to stay home and listen to Kathy's stories.

"Just imagine, Jerry. Our living master, here in the flesh, and we have the opportunity to meet him." Her voice flowed with gratitude and awe. I had heard her speak many times about her personal contact with Maharaj Ji. Now, when she had just returned and I was just getting ready to go, the enormity of this opportunity sank in. I was going to meet my master.

The more enthusiastic she was about her trip, the more anxious I was to start my own journey. However, on the day they left, David and Kathy learned that Maharaj Ji would be traveling and would not be at the village when I arrived. Instead of waiting in an ashram in India without him, I decided to delay my departure. I changed my plane reservation so I could stay here in the house for an additional week.

It was a wonderful week. Kathy's stories about India reminded me of the ones she told in her book, in which she described her visit to the village in the early sixties. Back then, only a dozen or fewer people from the West met in an intimate setting in Maharaj Ji's rose garden. Since that time, the teachings had become more popular and to accommodate the increased interest, there was now a large hostel for Western visitors. Kathy and David told me what to expect, where to go for Indian clothing, and how wonderful it was to be in Maharaj Ji's presence. By the end of the week, I felt closer to both of them than ever.

In addition to her exuberance about Maharaj Ji, Kathy had spells of sadness. "I hated leaving him," she said, her face drained of blood. "I don't know if I'll ever see him again."

She played a recording over and over, in which Roberta Flack sang about her love for a man who was killing her softly with his song. Those lyrics captured perfectly the mixing together of song and absolute love. It was just like the Path. We reached toward an audible God. We even used the word "Shabd" to indicate God, a word that could also be translated simply as "song." The lyrics and melody of "Killing Me Softly with His Song" communicated the Path as clearly as any words I had heard, conveying how love for the sound of God could penetrate the heart and transcend the ego.

When I was finally ready to go, Kathy gave me a letter to hand to Maharaj Ji when I had my interview with him. She said, "All of his mail is opened by his secretaries. This is the only way to communicate with him directly." Finally, it was time to go. David drove me to Newark Airport, and I began the long flight to India.

Killing Me Softly

India, 1975

I looked out the window of the plane as we crossed over the infinite darkness of the Atlantic Ocean. Since I first read Kathy's book four years ago, I had longed to meet the living master in person. Now, at last, I was on my way. The sense of being aloft and the drone of the engines stole my sense of time. I attempted to say my mantra as continuously as possible, dozed off, or read a few passages from the book about the Path that I kept open on my lap.

During a stop in the Middle East I stayed in my seat, looking out at soldiers on the tarmac. Their automatic weapons reminded me I was passing through parts of the world where life was very different from that with which I was familiar.

Twenty-four hours after leaving home, I arrived in India. After having meditated and snoozed for so long, when I deplaned among Indians in exotic garb, speaking in lovely, enticing accents, I imagined they were all related in some way to Maharaj Ji and the Path.

Outside, the air was alive with the exotic smells of incense and food. I plopped my suitcase in front of the cabstand and gave the cabbie the address. Soon we entered what appeared to be a carnival. In the gathering dusk, I looked out at the masses of Indians and imagined each one as a soul on a journey. Eventually, I gave up, leaned back against the seat, closed my eyes and repeated my mantra.

When we pulled up to our destination, I was surprised to see we were in front of a camera store. Inside was a large room with glass display cases filled with cameras and photography accessories. Several assistants looked busy, cleaning everything with an urgency that seemed out of place, considering I was the only visitor. A clean-shaven Indian man dressed in Western clothing emerged from the back. Instead of offering me the warm welcome I expected, he said, "Where have you been? You're late."

"Sorry," I said, unsettled by his brusque attitude. "Since he was traveling I decided to delay my arrival."

"He changed his plans," he said. "He is there now. You must continue your journey immediately."

Realizing I had missed precious days with my guru, I shared this man's sense of urgency. He called an assistant to drive me to the train station. Neither the storeowner nor the driver asked for any money and I didn't offer any. Another journey through the city, then a wait in line for a train. Each step brought me closer.

On board, when I handed my ticket to the conductor, I asked him to help me get off at the right stop. He smiled and nodded, cordially reassuring me he would do so. I meditated and dozed as we pulled into station after station, approaching the northwest border of India. I occasionally tried to follow our progress on the map, but each station seemed the same as the last. I turned my attention inward, to the rhythm of saying the mantra, lulled by the clickety-clack and the swaying of the train. I snapped to attention when the conductor touched me on the shoulder, warning me that we were approaching my stop. I gathered my things and got off at the tiny rural station.

The train pulled away leaving me alone on a platform lit only by a few bulbs. I wondered how I would go the rest of the way.

Jerry Waxler

After a few minutes, a man approached, smiling and placing his palms together. Relieved, I returned the greeting. He said he would drive me to the village. I settled into his car, my excitement and fatigue competing for my attention. After a few miles of bumpy roads, we pulled up to the village gates where the guards waved us through.

When the car stopped, I was surprised that there was no receiving desk or any procedure for ushering me in. The driver asked around and finally he found a man who knew what to do. This other man smiled and led me through a corridor and up one flight of stairs to my room. It had unadorned walls, a high ceiling, two beds, a wardrobe for my clothes and a private bathroom. I lay down, exhausted and disoriented. "I'm in India, now," I thought. "The land of my guru."

Somewhere in the distance I heard a song playing. At first I couldn't identify the sound and was surprised that in this place of meditation there would be any noise late in the evening when I expected everyone to be in bed. Then I recognized the song. It was Roberta Flack singing the same song Kathy had been playing in the house the day before I left Pennsylvania.

I listened to the lyrics about a lover who was "strumming my pain" and "singing my life" and I started to sob. This musical link between Kathy and my guru seemed prophetic, uncanny. This song, in this place, synthesized everything I had been feeling. If I was ever going to penetrate the mystery of life, this was the time.

Too restless to sleep, I left my room, feeling like a thief trying to steal a glimpse of the spirituality that must be all around. I ventured onto the walkway. The song was no longer playing, but I walked toward a group of people on the far side of the courtyard. They were gathered around a doorway that opened

200

into a community room packed with people dressed in formal Indian attire, the men in fine jackets, most in turbans, and the women in saris, an explosion of color and fashion.

I asked a bearded man who looked like he might be guarding the door, "What is happening here?"

He said in British-accented English, "It's a wedding. Maharaj Ji's son is getting married." It was a family affair of course, but I couldn't resist the pressure of curiosity. I asked the man if I could poke my head in. By this time my beard was growing out, and my hair was long and disheveled, and I took no particular care with my clothes, but he didn't seem to mind. He smiled and said, "Yes, of course."

I stood near the entrance looking around the noisy room, above the heads of people packed shoulder to shoulder. On a raised platform, several people sat clothed in garb so elaborate they looked like royalty. And there he was, looking out over the crowd. After four years of staring at Maharaj Ji's photos, I was seeing him in person. I had to adjust my vision to see his form in three dimensions. After a few moments of total absorption, I felt a pang of self-consciousness. This was a private affair and I probably should leave.

As I stood outside, not sure what to do next, I heard a commotion. Maharaj Ji was leaving the party and coming my way. I waited on the sidewalk along with a few dozen Indian well-wishers. When he passed, I felt a crazy compulsion. In the books about following a spiritual teacher, there were many stories about devoted disciples hurling themselves upon the guru's mercy, begging him to accept them. Inspired by those images, I fell into step behind him.

The other people in the crowd gasped at my effrontery. This man was revered by hundreds of thousands of people throughout India and around the world, and a stranger was invading his personal space. But instead of worrying about the gasps, I felt relief. Here I was, in this private compound on the outskirts of a tiny village in northwest India, and I was following my teacher on the path.

After a few steps, he turned around to look at me. I wasn't sure what to expect. Perhaps he might say something like "Ah, my old friend. You've come at last." What he did say surprised me and penetrated deep into my mind. He said in a firm voice, "Go do your work." Then he turned around and walked away. I stood there in a daze. I had met my teacher, and he told me to get busy growing. It was perfect. He was killing me softly.

Life at the Spiritual Village

I returned to my room, eager to meditate. The area on the floor next to the wall would do. Here I was at last. When I closed my eyes, I tried to visualize his presence, as I had been taught at initiation. When I grew too tired, I leaned over and passed out. A few hours later, I was roused from slumber by a loud clap of thunder. I lay awake listening to long, low-throated rumbles, full of texture, like whale songs, that went on and on.

I faded again, and at three a.m. was jolted awake by sirens sounding throughout the village to signal the morning meditation. Kathy and David had warned me about these. Once I got over the surprise, I felt comforted by the morning call to meditation, knowing I was in India with my master, at his spiritual village.

I sat on the floor with my legs crossed. When I became too tired I slumped back against the wall, continuing to silently repeat my mantra. After the prescribed two and a half hours, I stood up and looked out into the courtyard, lush with exotic trees and shrubs. I went back into my room for another hour and dozed and meditated some more. The next time I looked at my clock, it was time for breakfast.

Following other Western guests, I found the dining hall where forty or fifty people, almost all dressed in Western clothes, were already seated at small tables. I sat by myself, saying my mantra and waiting patiently for one of the waiters to bring me the dish they were serving. I enjoyed the savory Indian food, surprisingly mild compared with the food Sanjay's wife had served. And I avoided conversation with any of the other guests. When I was finished, I asked a man who seemed to be in charge what the schedule was. He said that in a couple of hours Maharaj Ji would be giving a *satsang* in the local Indian dialect.

I walked out of the walled guest compound, down dirt and brick streets to visit the shops that Kathy and David had told me about. Unlike the streets I had passed on my way from the airport, these were clean and quiet, with no beggars and only a few cars.

I intended to purchase a woolen shawl like the one I had for years seen draped over Maharaj Ji's shoulders. Made of finely spun wool, the garment had come to symbolize life at the spiritual village, and I wanted one of my own. Kathy and David also suggested I buy a lightweight pajama-like outfit, called a *salwar kameez*, which I could wear around the village.

The population in the village was limited to followers of the Path, and as I walked I caught the eyes of passersby and pressed my hands together in greeting, knowing we were all here for one thing, to be near our master. Only a few blocks away, I stood at the tailor's tiny stall communicating with gestures and a few words of English. Like the people I passed on my walk around the village, the tailor was polite and smiled frequently and openly. As he took my measurements, his attention made me feel welcome. The shawl and pajamas cost only a fraction of what I would pay for clothing at home. He said I could pick them up later in the week.

The morning *satsang* was held in the courtyard of the beautiful Satsang Hall, constructed like something in a Persian fantasy, with spires and porticoes. Once, at a meeting at Sanjay's, someone read us a story about how, when the architect who designed this building needed to clarify a detail, he asked his spiritual teacher, who opened the architect's inner vision so he could see similar buildings in higher regions of consciousness. The rest of us expected to meditate for a lifetime in order to pass through such ethereal regions on our way back to God consciousness. So hearing about this architect being given a free ride sent us into peels of laughter.

I sat with the other Westerners, cross-legged on a mat just in front of the dais where Maharaj Ji would sit. As I gazed up at the platform, waiting for him to arrive, I glanced back at the hundreds of Indians seated behind me and wondered if they minded our privileged position. When he entered, I forgot my concerns.

He sat cross-legged on a raised platform, and I studied his face. He was handsome, with a high forehead, a long beard, and a relaxed manner. I stared at him with all my might, hoping that through sheer force of will I could follow him more closely.

A singer, called a *pathi,* began a haunting singsong chant. These chants were taken from a variety of religious sources, such as from the Sikh and Hindu scriptures and from writings of the Sufi mystics. Above Maharaj Ji, brilliant green parrots flitted and sang amid the decorative scrollwork at the top of the portico.

When the *pathi* fell silent, Maharaj Ji spoke. His voice was melodious, rich, and rhythmic as if halfway between speaking and singing. I felt a thrill of delight when a few English words emerged. He quoted the passage in the Christian Bible, "If thine eye be single, thy whole body shall be full of light." I had seen this phrase quoted many times in books about the Path. This is how Jesus taught his disciples to meditate on the Third Eye, the same method for enlightenment that had been passed down in secret from master to disciple through the ages.

I smiled at the cosmic irony: I was a Jew listening to my Indian master giving me the same instructions Jesus gave his disciples two thousand years ago. I couldn't decide if that made me Christian. Or did it make me a Sikh? Or was I still really a Jew? All my life I had been horrified by the slaughter of innocents that had been justified by the dangerous business of quoting from the wrong scripture, or even quoting the same scripture but interpreting it differently. In this moment, listening to these quotes from Jesus as well as from religious teachers throughout history, I felt so profoundly grateful to be learning about God from a man who believed we are all one.

According to some estimates, Maharaj Ji had 600,000 followers around the world, and as a result, few of us expected to have much time with him. These visits from Westerners provided an exceptional opportunity, not only to stay at the spiritual village, but even more personally, to have a brief interview when we arrived and when we left. Later that day, we lined up, waiting our turn. When I sat down next to him, just the two of us, I felt incredibly awkward. After saying hello, I handed him the letter Kathy had given me. When he finished reading it, I told him about the small community that had gathered around Kathy at the house.

He looked at me and asked, "How are the people at the house?"

At that moment, I noticed his eyes were brilliant blue. *That's not possible. They're brown, right?* I looked more closely, and the blue opened up deeper and deeper, as if his eyes were an ocean and I was diving in. My soul swooned into his, distracted only by the expanse of his forehead, which seemed at that moment to fill the sky. Within a split second the sensation was over.

I have always cherished moments of deep eye contact, thinking of them as the ultimate intimacy. Occasionally a shared glance with a stranger elicited the feeling that our souls had accidentally leapt across the distance that separated us. I savored any moment when energy jumped between two people, carried by a glance. But there was an added dimension in the energy that crossed between this older man and me, an uplifting relief that I never knew about and didn't expect. My first mystical experience took place inside Maharaj Ji's eyes.

Meetings for Westerners

Even though I sat at a table by myself in the dining room, I couldn't escape the nervous energy I felt when around so many people. So I began to avoid the dining hall altogether. Instead, I bought food from street vendors outside the walls of the guest compound. I felt more peaceful among the locals. I hoped to blend in by wearing my newly purchased *salwar kameez* and shawl. The Indians all looked wise, with their dark skin, melodic voices and exotic clothes. I wondered how long they had been following Maharaj Ji.

I occasionally sat and read a few passages from the spiritual books I always carried. From these passages, I continued to learn the similarity between Maharaj Ji's teachings and the teachings of other holy men and women throughout history. Their words always brought me peace.

When I returned to the guesthouse, I went straight to my room, wiling away hours by meditating and writing letters to Kathy on the powder blue airmail letter paper. Writing to her helped me establish a link between my two most spiritual places, home and northwest India.

After dinner, I attended a meeting conducted in English. These meetings were similar to the ones I read about in Kathy's book. Back in 1960, the period she had written about, a handful of Western visitors sat with Maharaj Ji in his rose garden. In the intervening fifteen years, the Path had become better known in the West, and as a result, during my visit, sixty or more people met in a more formal meeting room.

Following my pattern of avoiding people, I slipped into a seat at the last minute. Each night the meeting started with a talk by an elderly Indian man who introduced himself as Professor Bhatnagar. His stiff posture and stern, commanding voice gave the impression that it would be easy to annoy him. He almost seemed mildly annoyed just standing there. Once someone asked him a question, and he blurted out, "You Westerners will never understand."

Even though he was crabby, I liked Professor Bhatnagar. He was old enough to have been initiated by Maharaj Ji's grandfather and when he spoke I heard echoes from those years. I listened to his discourse with my eyes closed and with my shawl pulled up over my head. With the fabric draped over my face, I disappeared into myself. The passages from various mystics reiterated the basic message of the Path. If you meditate and trust the master, you will gradually merge with God.

On nights when Maharaj Ji strode in, a sigh went through the room. Turning to us briskly, with palms pressed together in greeting, he mounted the stage, and sat on a comfortable looking chair. We then had the opportunity to ask questions.

Since the meditation took place within our own minds, many obscure, imprecise questions arose. "Exactly where am I supposed to focus?" "What if my body doesn't feel right?" "What if my mind is agitated?" For years I had seen his responses in the books, but no matter how many times he answered, disciples came up with new ways to ask the same questions. Now that I was in his presence, I listened carefully to his turn of phrase, the tone in his voice, and any other indications that might add to the insights I had already gleaned. The most wonderful thing about listening in person was tuning into the kindness and supportiveness in his voice.

One woman complained about the difficulty of finding time to meditate.

"Sister. Slowly and slowly, you will feel God's love when you close your eyes," Maharaj Ji said. "When you begin to experience that love, you will long to meditate and will run toward it."

Another man said even when he meditated, he couldn't stop worrying. Maharaj Ji replied, "Repeat your mantra with love, and your loving attention will help lift you."

This emphasis on love was difficult for me. My whole life, I had focused more on ideas than on emotions. I studied ideas, thought about ideas, and even felt my feelings through ideas. Now I was being asked to experience love, but if there was a spigot that would turn on the flow, I couldn't find the handle. Sitting in his presence, I figured this was my chance to ask.

I raised my hand, and when his assistant called on me, I said, "Maharaj Ji, you say to do the meditation with love, but I don't understand. What exactly am I supposed to love?"

A few disapproving gasps erupted from the audience, as if I had asked something stupid or insolent. I knew very well that I was supposed to feel love for the master. I did feel a total devotion to his ideas, and felt an extraordinary appreciation for the mission of this man who had committed his life to training me to grow closer to God. I just wanted to know how to proceed.

He looked at me with eyes full of compassion and I looked at him across the room, wondering what he would say. In that moment our eyes locked as if we were the only two people there. He didn't seem concerned about my strange appearance or intense manner. In his beautiful, rumbling, slow voice he said, "Love the mantra."

His gentle smile set me at ease and, as his answer sunk in, it was my turn to gasp. *Of course. It makes perfect sense.* I had always loved words. When I tried to learn new things, or make sense of the world, I turned to words to help. Now, he was drawing my attention to the fact that these were the words I had been looking for all my life, the key to opening up the prison of my mind, to let go all those thoughts and to leave them all behind.

"Thank you, Maharaj Ji," I said, flooded with gratitude to this kind man who in so few words, had eased my worries and lifted my burdens. I asked him about love and he lovingly answered, making his own love available to me and reassuring me that my agitated, overly intellectual mind was not going to interfere with our agreement to find a personal connection to God.

Seva

Despite my general preference to keep to myself, one afternoon I decided to attend *seva,* an opportunity for anyone at the spiritual village to perform simple menial service to help maintain the village. One such activity was "brick *seva.*" I had seen photos of brick *seva,* showing groups of people kneeling on the ground, striking bricks with small hammers. It looked like a perfect opportunity to repeat my mantra and contribute to the upkeep of the village.

After lunch, I joined a dozen people who sat on their haunches or kneeled in front of piles of old bricks. These bricks had originally been fashioned from clay taken out of the riverbed, and fired in a kiln fueled by marsh grass taken from the riverbanks. The bricks were then used in the construction of homes and common buildings, as well as the ten-foot-high wall around the perimeter of the village. Whenever the boundaries of the village grew, sections of the wall were knocked down and the bricks were carted here for recycling.

The bricks were brittle, so it only took a few blows for me to shatter each one. I tossed the resulting chips on a pile. The rubble would be used as landfill when constructing streets.

Despite the fact that Westerners were typically separated from Indians, a dark-skinned woman in a sari broke bricks nearby. When she said hello to me in English I felt a tug in my heart. She was young and attractive and obviously comfortable speaking to

Westerners. Overriding my typical shyness, I wanted to know more about her.

Pausing from my task, I asked, "Where are you from?"

"I just returned from the States. I went to college in California," she said. I loved the comfortable sound of her voice.

"What brings you here?" I asked.

"My father is a retired engineer," she said. "He built a house here at the village."

The longer we talked, the more comfortable I became. I loved her accent. I loved her eyes. And her father was an insider. My mind exploded with the possibilities. I fantasized about how much fun it would be to spend more time with her. She could show me around the village, from an insider's vantage point. Maybe we were right for each other. I had heard of an American disciple who had made an arranged marriage with a lovely Indian woman. Perhaps this was the way out of my impasse with relationships. I asked her if I could see her again, and she seemed as curious about me as I was about her. We made plans to meet the next day.

When the appointed time came, she showed up only long enough to tell me that her parents forbade her from seeing me. They wanted her to marry an Indian and did not see the point in her hanging around with a Westerner. She apologized and looked resigned. There was really nothing she could do. She hoped I understood.

I did understand, but it hurt anyway. I imagined myself through their eyes, with my bushy beard and furtive ways. Even if they didn't mind me being a Westerner, I was only an engineer, and barely that. What prospects did I have to offer? I retreated back into my isolated routine.

During one evening meeting, Professor Bhatnagar announced that a *bhandara* would begin the following week. Several times each year, disciples from all over the country descended on this small town to attend Maharaj Ji's discourse. I had seen photos of these gatherings and I was looking forward to experiencing this for myself.

For days, people poured in on foot. Arriving buses and trucks overflowed with passengers hanging on the sides or sitting on the roof. Most of the visitors remained outside the walls of the town, camping in tents set up for them in the surrounding fields.

When it was time to assemble, ushers guided us Westerners to our place at the front of a crowd so vast that individuals in the back were like distant dots—which meant that to them, Maharaj Ji must have been barely visible. I worried for them and was in awe of the devotion that motivated them to come all the way here. Why were we Westerners so spoiled? But when we were being led to our spots, I saw that for this large gathering, row upon row of impeccably dressed Indian dignitaries were seated in front of us. Maybe we weren't so special after all.

I imagined a reverse pecking order that gauged material wealth going from front to back and spiritual longing going in the other direction. Those in the back were perhaps the most devoted of all, willing to undergo days of hardship in exchange for a glimpse, and those in front had the biggest egos and had to be treated delicately to avoid offending them. Perhaps this was Maharaj Ji's gentle way of letting me see how on a scale of humility, I still had a long way to go.

When Maharaj Ji climbed the stairs to the dais, a distinguished looking man in a white turban and long beard followed him and sat slightly behind him and off to his side, quietly gazing out over the crowd.

The meetings started with a *pathi* chanting from scriptures, much like the cantor who sings alongside the Rabbi in a Jewish service. When the chanting was finished, Maharaj Ji began his discourse. Since he spoke in a foreign language, I focused my attention on his rhythmic voice.

Out of the unintelligible syllables emerged an English phrase, "God so loved the world, He sent His only begotten Son," a line that I found to be one of the most comforting in the whole teaching. The books explained that in every age, God places a representative on earth to help us find our way home. I closed my eyes to focus on the universal love that connects people of different religions. Instead of calling attention to the differences, Maharaj Ji always emphasized the similarities.

After the *satsang*, as I pushed through the crowd, a car slowly made its way past me. People were running up to the car and pressing their palms together in greeting. Inside the car was the man in the white turban who had been sitting next to Maharaj Ji. I asked someone standing near me who that was. He said with reverence, "That is a fully realized saint from a nearby village."

Cool! This was the man David and Kathy had told me about. He had his own disciples to whom he gave initiation and guidance, and yet, during large gatherings, Maharaj Ji invited him to share the dais.

That was so typical of the generous spirit of this Path. Instead of Maharaj Ji jealously guarding his supremacy and leading his followers to believe he was the only one, he invited this man to sit next to him. By doing so, he let us know that God so loved the world he sent more than one messenger.

Afterward, I followed the crowds to the communal kitchens where the ocean of disciples would be fed for free. I did not intend to eat there, but simply wanted to witness it. Hundreds of women sat on their haunches around fire pits, baking chapattis, while men stirred enormous vats of dal. A stream of servers ran back and forth, providing food to the endless rows of Indians sitting on mats. I would not have believed an operation of such magnitude could exist if I had not seen it for myself.

That afternoon I joined swarms of people, heading toward the hilly area adjoining the village. This uneven riverbed had been exposed when the river shifted course and every year, during the great gatherings, devotees moved dirt in order to level the land and make it useful.

The hard clay had been waterworn during the years it lay under the river, and exhibited the same soft appearance as the sand castles I built as a child on the beach at the Jersey shore. And like children, we moved toward the work site with as much joy as if we were going to a party.

As I drew closer, I passed people carrying baskets of earth balanced on top of their heads. I smiled and they were quick to meet my eyes and smile back. Eventually I reached my destination, a hill on which men and boys were hacking out chunks with shovels and filling baskets. One of the men saw that I didn't know what to do. He pointed to a pile of cloth rings, and gestured that I should place one on top of my head.

Then, a couple of guys lifted a basket of clay and placed it on the cloth ring, which cushioned my head as well as stabilized the load. I actually enjoyed the sensation. Compared with a yoga headstand, during which my head carried the full weight of my body, this basket felt light.

I started back, following others also carrying baskets on their heads. When we reached the gully that needed to be filled, we leaned forward and threw the baskets forward. More men and boys moved the clay into place with hoes.

Maharaj Ji looked down over us, sitting under an umbrella to protect him from the sun, with a few people seated on the ground around him. A flood of devotion flowed through me—a connection with him and these hundreds of thousands of fellow disciples. The single reason we were all here today was to be closer to this man and to figure out some way to serve him. Moving dirt was the best way for now, so I moved dirt.

Later that night, while waiting for Maharaj Ji to come and give our English language *satsang*, I heard two people behind me joking about dirt *seva*. One of them told the story in the Bible in which Jesus was being served dinner. While Martha worked in the kitchen, Mary sat and stared at Jesus. Later, when the workingwomen complained about Mary's behavior, Jesus defended her and said her devotion was a worthwhile form of service.

The next day, feeling sore and tired, I decided to follow Mary's example. Instead of joining the work crew, I would sit up on the hill next to Maharaj Ji. I saw other Westerners do it and I had never heard of any of them being chased away. When I approached, his assistants didn't stop me. I joined the small group sitting near him, and silently continued to seek deeper insight in the presence of this person who had offered me so much.

The backdrop to my view of Maharaj Ji were the thousands of volunteer laborers carrying dirt from one location and dumping it at another, in service to him. At first I saw it as an act of selfless devotion. And then, the scene blurred and I saw that it was not much different from the rivers of students I passed on my way to classes, or the rivers of hippies I passed in Berkeley, or the rivers of workers I passed on the streets of Philadelphia. We were all

Jerry Waxler

going from one point to the next in order to shift our own little bit of earth.

I was glad to be here for now, learning how to be devoted to him. I hoped that when I went home, I could be as graceful and matter-of-fact about moving my own bit of earth, day after day, year after year, while at the same time remembering this moment on the hill and understanding I was doing it all for God.

The Departure

I felt so grateful that I had met a teacher who would help me return to God. And yet I couldn't help wishing I had been just a little luckier. My teacher lived thousands of miles away and had a half-million disciples. I might never see him again. I wished I could have been born into a situation where I could spend a lot more time with him, learning not just from afar, but from his eyes, and advice, and presence.

My letters to Kathy began to include worries about reentering the world. I didn't want to lose the magic I felt here. When I received her reassuring words, I laughed at myself. How silly of me to think that God's love only exists in India. God's love is inside us, not in buildings, ashrams, or countries. But still I hoped that fact would stay with me when I was in Pennsylvania. I felt so grateful that I had formed this connection with Kathy. Life at home seemed a lot less bleak when I thought about returning to be around her.

Near the end of my stay, Kathy wrote to say that she and David were remodeling part of their house and the renovation would include a room for me. She asked me if I wanted to live there. I sat with the letter, thrilled they would make such a generous offer and relieved that I would have a safe place to land. I wrote back thanking her and telling her what a comfort and honor it would be. "Thank you. Thank you. Thank you." The offer quelled my rising concern about how I was going to fit into my old life. With their support, I would be able to follow the Path while living in the world.

When it came time to retrace my journey, I was at peace. I had one last meeting with Maharaj Ji. His greatness filled the air, leaping across the space between us. His sonorous voice and high forehead lifted me, and even though we only exchanged a few formal words, I felt like everything in my life was going to work out.

§§§

Emerging from the train into the New Delhi station, I pushed through the throng of passengers, vendors, beggars, and baggage carriers. Welcome back to civilization. Trying to cling to my inner peace amid this feverish tempest of humanity, I slid into a cab, closed the door behind me, and sighed with relief.

But it was not so easy to escape. Each time we stopped at a traffic light, dozens of children, many of them blind or deformed, crowded against the window to plead for money. I closed my eyes, trying to shut out the horror. All these desperate people — who will help them? How will their lives ever change?

I cried out to Maharaj Ji to teach me how to love them without feeling smothered by their pain. I imagined him by my side saying, in a sorrowful voice, "Suffering is part of this world. The only relief for any of us is to return to our true home."

The perspective helped me accept them, not as frightening apparitions, but as fellow souls, on a horrifying leg of the same journey we are all traveling. Just a couple of years earlier, my own choices brought me dangerously close to being a beggar myself. Now I realized that my plan to move to the jungle would have simply traded one set of desires for another. After a few months scrounging for food on the beach, I would have hated the endless discomfort of sand and hunger, and envied the tourists who could return to their hotel rooms. Whether on the beach or in an office, I was stuck on the same spinning globe, never satisfied, always seeking.

The taxi picked up speed and we cruised past people hurrying from one place to another, similar to the crowds I had seen all over the world. Despite differences in clothing, skin color, or language, our souls longed for the same thing.

Perhaps visionary author Marshall McLuhan was right. Perhaps the whole world was turning into one village. But he was mistaken when he said that technology caused our sense of togetherness. After three months in India I realized the sense of familiarity we felt for each other originated not from the glimpses we saw on screens, but from the longings that emerged from deep within our souls.

I remembered the story Kathy told about driving with Maharaj Ji at the New Jersey shore. "Look Maharaj Ji, there's a church on the right and a cemetery on the left." At first I thought his suggestion to "go straight ahead into the ocean" was a perfect metaphor for steering between organized religion and death. Now I expanded my vision and realized his witty comeback explained my entire life.

In high school, my future seemed obvious. To connect with the world, all I needed to do was climb to the top of society and become a doctor. But when I understood the horror of war, I turned away from my ambition and fought against money and power with all my might. No matter how hard I rebelled, I couldn't quell the fire burning in my heart.

After failing to find peace by moving toward society or away from it, I thought I had run out of options. In my desperation, the Path offered a third direction. Instead of going right or left, I could follow Maharaj Ji's advice and go straight ahead into the ocean of love.

Jerry Waxler

According to mystics, we are all drops in one ocean, and as we grow closer to God, we become increasingly aware of the God in each other. That was the basis for the greeting, *Namaste*. I bow to the God within you. Looked at individually, the gesture was an ancient, peaceful salutation between two people. But now, people around the world were feeling it en masse, and as a result the walls that separated us were crumbling before our eyes. I was returning to the U.S. not as an American or as a Jew, but as a soul on a journey, and everyone, no matter how they dressed or where they lived, was on the journey with me.

Life in Pennsylvania

The bright lights of Newark Airport dazed me as I disembarked. My life seemed fractured between the ashram in remote India, heading back to an office in Philadelphia. And yet I trusted that my spiritual unfolding would lead me exactly where I needed to go.

I made my way through customs, wondering who from the house would come to pick me up. And then, there she was. Kathy herself.

"Welcome home!" she said.

I hugged her. "What a relief to see you! Thank you so much for coming to pick me up."

Another one of our band of meditators, Bill, had driven her. He gave me a big booming hello, and another hug.

"Let me look at you," Kathy said. "I can feel the love Maharaj Ji sent back with you."

I could feel it too, and I hoped somehow I could hold onto it forever. On the way home, she asked me to tell her about Maharaj Ji, and I repeated what I said in the letter, that he asked me how people were at the house. She laughed and said she was so glad I would be moving in. During the drive we grew quiet, and in the silence, I repeated my mantra, now lifted by the joy of being home and the gratitude for all that had happened.

After two hours, we pulled into the long dirt driveway, past bushes and large trees to the house in the woods. When David heard us arrive, he ran outside to greet us. With his broad smile he said, "Welcome to your new home, brother."

He gestured to the front of the house. What had been the door of a two-car garage when I left for India was now an exterior wall with a regular entry door. We entered a new kitchen, with an island in the middle.

"What are those benches?" I asked, pointing to the seating at the kitchen table.

"Old church pews we found at an auction," David said. I laughed at the irony. Sitting on a hard wooden pew every day seemed like a nice touch.

"We didn't do so well with the table." He jiggled the top and it teetered. "We ran out of money."

Passing through the kitchen to what had been the other half of the garage, he showed me my room. It was furnished with a handmade bed constructed from unstained lumber, with a thick foam mat on top. It looked more comfortable than anything I'd slept on in years. "Thanks, David. This is incredible."

He pointed to the wall between my room and the kitchen. "We constructed the wall with staggered studs to insulate you from the noise."

I breathed a sigh of relief. When I meditated, I craved solitude and the thought had crossed my mind that being this close to the kitchen had some disadvantages.

"That's going to help a lot."

I walked over to the small window that looked out onto the driveway. On the sill, a plant grew in a translucent green bottle filled with water.

Kathy said, "I picked this out just for you."

I touched its fleshy leaves, and said, "Hello, little friend. I guess we'll be roommates."

"Come on upstairs. We'll show you how big the living room is now that we moved the kitchen downstairs."

I wanted to sleep, and yet I was excited to be here. We walked upstairs to the living room, with its stone fireplace that reached up to the peak of the A-frame ceiling. Looking out the picture windows through the trees, I could see the small stream. I couldn't believe I was going to live here. I felt like I was in a dream.

After Bill drove away, I realized I had not seen any of the half-dozen people who were living here before I left for India. "Where is everyone?"

"Each of them found somewhere else to go," Kathy said.

"Oh, that's too bad. I was looking forward to living in a community."

"Don't worry," she said. "Maharaj Ji says that when we are born, we're like birds landing on a tree. We chatter and flock together and when it's time to move on, we fly away. Soon a new flock will appear." I liked the analogy. The flock had moved on. I wondered what the new flock would be like.

When the tour was over, I went downstairs and sat on the bed, exhausted from the trip, and leaned against the wall to silently repeat my mantra. Now that I had met Maharaj Ji in person, I could feel his presence with me.

§§§

Over the next couple of days I recovered from the plane ride but not from the disorientation. I still wanted to be in India, with my teacher, and if I couldn't be there, I wanted to stay in this house and meditate.

I knew I had to make a living, but how would I cope with the pressures of going into the city every day? I had to talk myself through my worry. *Trust God*, I repeated to myself when the worry seemed too much to bear.

David helped me start my car after its long hibernation. My first trip was to the train station to pick up a schedule. I walked up to the ticket window, my heart pounding, wondering how in the world I would find the courage to return to the working life. *The long train ride will be a good opportunity to say my mantra*, I told myself, trying to feel brave.

I had two weeks until my leave of absence ran out. For now, I would enjoy these precious moments. Every day I meditated for hours. When I heard Kathy playing the piano, I went upstairs and listened. Her music combined with my gratitude, transforming the repetition of my mantra into a great cosmic dance.

When she returned to her writing, I walked out to the woods. Wind whispered through the leaves, as if the trees knew I had fallen in love with God. Behind the house, I gently pushed aside the bushes crowding the narrow path and made my way down toward the stream, stopping for a moment to watch a chipmunk scurry through the underbrush. The babbling of water grew louder as I approached, and then louder still at my favorite spot, near a drop where the water splashed and tumbled across the rocks. Sitting in a cross-legged pose, I watched the water flow by. Then I closed my eyes and repeated my mantra, listening carefully for the sound of God.

§§§

When I closed my eyes and listened to that babbling brook, I knew I had come home. I had found a place to live. I was ready to earn a living. And most important of all, I had become aware of the longing of my soul. With all these pieces in place, I had reached the end of one long journey and was about to start the next one.

David and Kathy turned out to be fanatical lifelong learners, studying system after system that would enable them to creatively engage with life. In the environment they provided, I explored a broad range of methods to grow, including dance and movement workshops, writing for healing, and talk therapy. I even came to see my career as an important part of my life, seeking jobs that would help me become a more complete person. By harnessing the same pressured, relentless questioning that had gotten me into my mental mess in the first place, I gradually climbed out.

It would be another seven years before I was mature enough to enter my first lasting relationship. Even after I was in a relationship, it would take more years of work to master the mutual respect and service that transforms sexual attraction into a lifelong partnership.

Eventually, I would return to school for a master's degree in counseling psychology. In my classes, instead of facing a blackboard and learning abstract ideas, we sat in a circle and removed the barriers between us. In those courses I learned that revealing secrets opens up authentic pathways among people. Above all, I learned the power of listening.

Before I enrolled in that program, I assumed I was lonely because people didn't "get" me. By the time I finished, I had learned the simple secret of harmony: In order to relate to people, I had to pay closer attention to them. Once I began to listen, the silence that had previously enveloped me was replaced with a symphony.

Famous Quotes: Life as a Story

"And when she buries a man, that action concerns me: all mankind is of one author, and is one volume; when one man dies, one chapter is not torn out of the book, but translated into a better language; and every chapter must be so translated; God employs several translators; some pieces are translated by age, some by sickness, some by war, some by justice; but God's hand is in every translation, and his hand shall bind up all our scattered leaves again for that library where every book shall lie open to one another." John Donne, 1623, *Devotions*

"The Body of B. Franklin, Printer. Like the Cover of an old Book, Its contents torn out. And Stript of Its Lettering & Gilding, Lies here. Food for Worms. But the Work shall not be lost. For it will as he believ'd appear once more In a new and more elegant Edition Corrected and Improved By the Author." Benjamin Franklin, *Epitaph*

"Behold the Child among his new-born blisses,
A six years' Darling of a pigmy size!
See, where 'mid work of his own hand he lies,
Fretted by sallies of his mother's kisses,
With light upon him from his father's eyes!
See, at his feet, some little plan or chart,
Some fragment from his dream of human life,
Shaped by himself with newly-learned art."

William Wordsworth, *Ode: Intimations of Immortality*

"It happens sometimes that I must say to a [...] patient: 'Your picture of God or your idea of immortality is atrophied, consequently your psychic metabolism is out of gear.'" Carl Jung, *Memories, Dreams, Reflections*

Jerry Waxler

Acknowledgments

The first hint I could make sense of my crazy years came from psychiatrist Lyndra Bills, who asked, "Have you ever placed events along a timeline?" The resulting chronological list shed light on what had until then been an unstructured morass. Several years later, I joined Foster Winans' writing community, where I discovered that writers help each other grow. In that magical environment, bestselling author Jonathan Maberry said, "It sounds like your ideas are dropping from the sky. Put in more of yourself." I realized that to find my own voice, I had to find my story.

Like an archeologist, I extracted fragments of my youth and lined them up. Critique partners—Flo Morton, Jennifer Lader, Melba Tolliver, Bill Weiser, and members of the Internet Writing Workshop—helped me turn glimpses into scenes and then into chapters.

As the manuscript matured, I received feedback from editors Emily Murphy, Susan Weaver, Lorraine Ash, Susan Gregory Thomas, Kerry Gans, Sharon Lippincott, Mike Ingram and Ruth Littner, from bookseller David Cronin, and from authors Julie Freed, Chuck Regan, Karen Swallow Prior, Tim Elhaj, and Linda Joy Myers. Special thanks to editor Kathryn Craft who shepherded it across the finish line.

Thanks to hundreds of memoir authors whose books gave me a crash course in turning life into story. And I acknowledge memoir readers who celebrate the universally known secret of human experience. We share the stage and we sit in the audience, simultaneously acting in our own dramas and watching each other. Welcome my friends to the show that never ends.

Made in the USA
Middletown, DE
14 December 2021

55754709R00130